CONTENTS

THE ALZHEIMER
SOCIETY of IRELAND

ACKNOWLEDGEMENTS

For any publishing project as special as this to see the light of day, it needs encouragement, expertise and advice from so many sources. From the day the project was first mooted, that support was there in abundance.
Thank you all so much.

A huge thank you to all the wonderful contributors – all the clients, carers, families, staff, volunteers and friends of ASI who submitted a recipe for consideration. Thank you for sharing your wonderful recipes and precious memories.

Thank you to Kate McCullough and Davina Smith for sharing their culinary expertise and testing the recipes. Cooks Academy Cookery School Dublin were so kind in allowing us the use of their premises for testing the recipes.

Big gratitude also to Anna Nowakowska of Matchbox Photography for her beautiful images and dedication to this project. It was a pleasure to work with you. The Mellow Fig and Bear Market Coffee provided us with the wonderful atmosphere and hospitality of their charming shops for the photography. Thank you to John Sutton for his guidance, expertise and enthusiasm and for helping to make this idea a reality. Finally, we received far more recipes and stories than we could fit in this publication, and of course multiple recipes for the same dish or bake – all of them truly worthy of inclusion.

We are heartbroken that we couldn't reproduce all the submissions, so a huge thank you to the contributors who have been so understanding of the limitations we faced.

Editor/Project Manager
Nikki Keegan

Book Design and Copy Editing
Persuasion Republic

Printers
Character Print

© Alzheimer Society of Ireland

Introduction

RECIPES FOR LOVE

Every classic dish, every new recipe, every culinary experiment began life as an idea, a question, a spark of imagination. Every great recipe began inside someone's head. But more importantly, it was born inside someone's heart. A recipe is a secret window to our experience, values and personality.

In fact, recipes, handed down from generation to generation, are little social histories. Memory triggers. Every recipe has a hidden love story.

Food gives us physical and social sustenance. And stories are the nutrition of life and conversation. This unique, collectible recipe book – *A Taste to Remember* – brings them both together, two rhyming and delicious ingredients – scrumptious homely recipes and memorable, moving stories.

This unique and beautiful cookbook is packed with personal, mouth-watering recipes and memorable stories from clients, families, staff and volunteers of The Alzheimer Society. We invited people from all around Ireland to share a precious recipe that reminded them of their childhood or a special time or place – and a revealing story behind the recipe. It also features recipes from Ireland's elite chefs including Darina Allen and Clodagh McKenna.

I'm sure you'll agree – the result is a wonder.

So dig in to this wondrous world of food, stories and love. You'll be physically nourished and emotionally enriched. And you'll be doing a truly remarkable thing for families living with Alzheimers and dementia.

Pat McLoughlin.

**Pat McLoughlin,
The Alzheimer Society of Ireland CEO**

THE STARTERS

MAMA SILVA'S ORGANIC VEGETABLE SOUP

From Silva Schawer, Rose Cottage, Co. Dublin

INGREDIENTS

- 2 tbsp of butter, for frying
- 3 organic vegetable stock cubes
- 1 tbsp of sugar
- Salt and pepper to season
- 2 leeks, only the white parts, washed and sliced
- 2–3 large organic potatoes, washed, peeled and diced
- 1 organic parsnip, washed, peeled and diced
- 750g organic carrots, washed, peeled and diced
- 1 organic turnip, washed, peeled and diced
- A small bunch of parsley
- 1–1.5 litres of water

METHOD

1. Melt the butter in a large pan, add the leeks and ⅓ of the carrots and fry for 5 minutes until soft.

2. Add 500ml of water, the sugar and the stock cubes and stir to dissolve the stock cubes.

3. Add the parsley, the rest of the vegetables and the rest of the water, a little at a time to make sure the pot is not too full and bring to a boil, stirring frequently.

4. Simmer for about 30 minutes until all the vegetables are cooked through, stirring every now and again.

5. Season with salt and pepper to taste.

6. Using a stick-blender or food processor, blend until smooth.

Serves: 10 portions – This soup can be frozen and defrosted as required and will keep in a fridge for a day as well.

STUFFED RASHER ROLL

From Katie Rael, Tralee Day Care Centre, Co. Kerry

INGREDIENTS

- 12 smoked back rashers (or unsmoked if preferred)
- 225g breadcrumbs
- 55g butter
- 1 large onion (finely chopped) and softened in some of the butter
- 1 heaped tbsp chopped fresh thyme
- 1 heaped tbsp chopped fresh parsley
- Salt and pepper to season (easy on the salt)

METHOD

"This recipe takes me back to the sunny Sunday lunch times of my childhood. On Saturdays, I would be sent to the pork butcher where I watched him expertly slice a pound of smoked back rashers from the whole side of bacon. Then it was into mother's herb garden for the fresh parsley and thyme, which was combined with melted butter, breadcrumbs, sautéed onions and salt and pepper (a small pinch of salt). This was spread along the length of the rashers which were then rolled neatly and baked (seam side down) for 15 to 20 mins at 200C, turning once. Then they were quickly flashed under a hot grill to crisp up (watch carefully!) and served up with Mam's crispy skin roast chicken and roast potatoes, with remaining stuffing on the side. It would, to quote the cook herself, 'warm the cockles of your heart'."

Serves: 6–8 people

SMOKED SALMON, LEMON AND DILL PÂTÉ

From Amy Vaughan, National Office, Dublin

INGREDIENTS

- 100g smoked salmon
- 100g cream cheese
- 1 tbsp horseradish sauce
- 1 lemon – for zest and juice
- 1 tsp fresh or dried dill
- 4 slices of bread, toasted
- Side salad to serve

METHOD

1. Place the smoked salmon and cream cheese in a blender and whizz until smooth.

2. Grate the lemon zest and add the juice of 1 lemon to the blender. Also add the dill and horseradish and blitz for 30 seconds. (Alternatively, you can finely chop the salmon and the dill, and mix everything together well, by hand.)

3. Place pâté in a bowl for serving, cover with cling film and chill for 20mins.

4. Cut bread into triangles or squares and toast before serving with pâté and a small side salad.

Serves: 4 people

CRAB SALAD WITH MANGO SALSA

From Maighread Ní Dhomhnaill Goan, National Helpline Volunteer, Dublin.

"Colette and I met as student nurses in the Mater Hospital in September 1972. We became great friends and although I shared a flat with my sister and brother, I frequently bunked in with Colette when we would be on long stints of night duty together. We've remained good friends since then and meet up regularly. Colette has done voluntary work all her life and it was she who introduced me to the Alzheimer Help Line where she has been working for some time. I introduced Colette to the magic of Crab from West Donegal and she shared her mushroom recipe the last time we had dinner in her home."

The Alzheimer National Helpline is a key part of the information services offered by The Alzheimer Society of Ireland. Set up in the year 2000, this free and confidential service provides practical information and emotional support to people with dementia and their families, to people who are concerned about their own or a family member's cognitive health and to professionals. The Helpline supports and empowers service users by providing quality information about dementia, about services and supports that may be available, and by providing a listening ear and a safe space to talk.

The Helpline service can be contacted by phone on **1800 341 341** or by email at **helpline@alzheimer.ie** and is open 6 days a week: between 10am–5pm Monday to Friday and 10am–4pm on Saturdays.

INGREDIENTS

Crab Salad
(Depending on how many people you're feeding)
* 1–2 containers of fresh crab meat (300– 400 Grams)
* 1 lime
* 1 large bunch of fresh coriander
* 1–2 tbsp mayonnaise
* Salt and pepper to taste

Mango Salsa
* 1–2 large ripe mangos
* 1 or 2 chillies
* 1 red onion
* 1 large lime
* 1 large bunch of fresh coriander
* Salt

METHOD

Crab Salad
* Mix the crab meat, zest and juice of one lime and finely chopped coriander (leaves only) in a bowl.
* Add – 1–2 tbsp mayonnaise.
* Salt and pepper to taste.

Mango Salsa
* Chop the mangos into a bowl.
* Add – 1 or 2 chillies deseeded and finely chopped, depending on taste.
* Add red onion finely chopped.
* Add large lime juiced and zest.
* Add one large bunch of fresh coriander – chopped.
* Season with salt to taste.

Serves: 2–3 people

STUFFED MUSHROOMS WITH GARLIC AND BACON

From Colette Moriarty, National Helpline Volunteer, Dublin.

This recipe was given to me by my friend Marie. It's a very popular starter with friends and family.

INGREDIENTS

- 4 large mushrooms
- 3tbsp olive oil
- 55g smoked bacon (diced)
- 2 cloves garlic crushed
- 55g breadcrumbs
- 55g ground almonds
- 2tbsp chopped basil
- 2tbsp cream
- 55g goats cheese (diced)
- 1 tbsp lemon juice
- Salt and pepper

METHOD

1. Preheat oven to 200°C.
2. Chop the mushroom stalks.
3. Heat 2tbsp of oil in a frying pan and add the mushroom stalks, bacon and garlic. Fry for 5 mins then transfer to a bowl.
4. Add the breadcrumbs, ground almonds, chopped basil, goats cheese, cream, lemon juice and seasoning. Mix well.
5. Divide between the mushroom caps.
6. Drizzle 1 tbsp of oil over the stuffed mushrooms and bake for 15 mins or until crisp.
7. Serve at once on a bed of leaves sprinkled with a good quality balsamic vinegar.

Serves: 3–4 people

TRADITIONAL POTATO CAKES

From Gerry Harney, Co. Kildare.

INGREDIENTS

- 1kg potatoes, peeled and boiled
- 1 egg
- 30g butter
- 2 tbsp flour
- Salt and pepper to taste
- 115g of diced cooked ham or smoked salmon

METHOD

1. Mash the hot boiled potatoes.
2. Add all the remaining ingredients and mix well.
3. Divide the mixture into eight or so portions and shape them into circles about one inch thick, putting them on floured plate as you go.
4. Fry in a cast iron pan over a medium heat until golden on both sides, using butter in the pan.

Serves: 8 people

CHILLI GARLIC SIZZLING PRAWNS

From Julie Mundy, Donegal.

INGREDIENTS

- 8 tbsp Donegal rapeseed oil
- 4 garlic cloves, thinly sliced
- 1 small red chilli, chopped
- 8 cherry vine tomatoes, halved
- 1kg king prawns, tails on
- 1 pinch of salt
- ¼ tsp paprika
- 3 tbsp white wine
- 2 tsp flat leaf parsley, chopped
- Juice from ¼ lemon

METHOD

1. Peel the prawns but leave the tails on and season with salt. Pour the Donegal rapeseed oil into a small frying pan and heat until simmering over a medium heat.

2. Add the chilli, garlic, cherry tomatoes and wine and sauté lightly for 2 minutes. Toss in the prawns and cook for 4 to 5 minutes, until they change colour and turn pink. Add a squeeze of lemon juice and the parsley and sprinkle with paprika.

3. Pour into a hot terracotta bowl and serve with warm crusty bread and lemon wedges.

Serves: 4 people

WARM BACON AND POTATO SALAD

From Julie Mundy, Donegal.

INGREDIENTS

- 1kg red potatoes, quartered
- 2 tbsp Donegal rapeseed oil
- 225g bacon, chopped into small pieces
- 1 clove of garlic, minced
- ½ red onion, chopped
- 1 stalk green onion, chopped
- Salt and pepper, to season
- Donegal rapeseed oil honey and mustard dressing

METHOD

1. Preheat oven to 180°C. On a baking sheet, toss the potatoes in Donegal rapeseed oil. Roast for 25 minutes or until tip of knife pierces potato easily. Heat a skillet on medium heat. Add the bacon and cook for 2 minutes. Then add in the garlic and red onion.

2. Sauté for additional 3 minutes until the bacon is crisp. Put the bacon, garlic and onions, including all of the bacon drippings, into a large bowl. Add in roasted potatoes and the green onions.

3. Season with salt and pepper and toss gently. Drizzle with Donegal rapeseed oil honey and mustard and serve immediately.

Serves: 6–8 people

POMEGRANATE AND BLUE CHEESE SALAD

From Martina Collins, Co. Clare

INGREDIENTS

- ½ cup pomegranate seeds
- ½ cup blue cheese – crumbled
- Handful of walnuts
- Romaine lettuce leaves
- Pinch of salt and pepper
- 2 tbsp extra virgin olive oil
- 2 tbsp balsamic vinegar
- Honey – to toast walnuts

METHOD

1. To make dressing, combine balsamic vinegar and oil and whisk well. Toast walnuts in honey under the grill for 3–4 minutes.
2. Place washed lettuce, pomegranate seeds and blue cheese in a large serving bowl, top with walnuts and dressing and add a pinch of salt and pepper to season.

Serves: 4 people

POACHED EGGS WITH COOLEA CHEESE AND COURGETTES

From Clodagh McKenna, Co. Cork

I am delighted to be supporting The Alzheimer Society of Ireland with this recipe. Their work within local communities is so important in order to help create a better way of life for those living with dementia or Alzheimer's.

INGREDIENTS

- 4 free range or organic eggs
- 1 courgette, sliced
- Olive oil
- 2 slices of sourdough toast
- Salt and pepper

For the Coolea cheese sauce:

- 100g Coolea cheese or gruyere
- 25g butter
- 25g flour
- 300ml milk
- Pinch of nutmeg
- Salt and white pepper

METHOD

How To Make Cheese Sauce:

1. Melt the butter in a saucepan and stir in the flour and cook for 1–2 minutes.
2. Then whisk in the milk to get a smooth sauce.
3. Simmer gently for 5 minutes and season with salt and white pepper.
4. Stir in cheese and nutmeg, allow to melt.

How To Poach An Egg:

1. Place a saucepan of salted water over a high heat and once the water has come to the boil give the water a good swirl using a spoon. Crack your eggs into a cup (one at a time) and bring the egg in the cup (one at a time) as close to the boiling water as possible and quickly drop the egg into the swirling water (the swirling water helps the white of the egg to form around the yolk.
2. Reduce the heat to medium and leave to cook for 3 minutes. Another trick is to add a generous amount of vinegar to the poaching liquid. This helps the eggs form into perfect spheres, BUT sometimes you can taste the vinegar in the eggs so the cupping method is what I suggest.
3. While the eggs are poaching, place a frying pan over a high heat and add 2 tablespoons of olive oil.
4. Once the oil is hot, tip in the courgettes and season with salt and pepper. Cook for a couple of minutes on each side.

Serves: 2 people

CRUSHED AVOCADO, BUCKWHEAT AND CITRUS FRUIT SALSA

From Brooks Hotel

Brooks Hotel has proudly supported The Alzheimer Society of Ireland as our Charity of Choice for 2016 and 2017. It is a charity that is close to the hearts of many of the team at Brooks Hotel.

Patrick, our Head Chef at Brooks Hotel decided to create a light, casual dish that is easy to make but most importantly is delicious and great to share with family and friends.

INGREDIENTS

- 75gm roasted buckwheat
- 150ml water
- Pinch salt and white pepper
- 1 tablespoon of olive oil
- 1 ruby grapefruit – peeled and segmented
- 1 orange – peeled and segmented
- 25gm red onion – finely chopped
- 1 vine tomato – halved, deseeded and finely chopped
- 20gm honey
- 20ml olive oil
- ½ teaspoon sea salt
- ½ teaspoon cracked black pepper
- 20gm toasted pumpkin seeds
- 1 avocado
- 1 lime
- Some shoots, sprouts or micro leaves to garnish

METHOD

For the Buckwheat: Steep the buckwheat in a ½ litre of cold water for ten minutes then rinse. Place the buckwheat into a small pot and place on a low heat, add the olive oil and a pinch of sea-salt & white pepper to season, then add the 150ml of water and bring to a boil, stirring well. Once boiled, remove from the heat, cover with a tight lid and leave to absorb the liquid. Once the liquid has been absorbed, spoon onto a shallow dish and cool completely. This can be done the day before and stored sealed in a container in the fridge.

For the Citrus Fruit Salsa: Place the segments of orange and grapefruit into sieve to drain off any excess liquid. In a separate bowl mix the red onion, chopped tomato, honey and olive oil, add a ½ teaspoon of sea-salt and ½ teaspoon of cracked black peppercorn and juice from ½ a lime. Give the segments a shake and add to this mixture, don't worry about breaking them.

For the Toasted Pumpkin Seeds: Put the pumpkin seeds onto a flat tray and place under a pre-heated grill. Keep an eye on them and once they start to pop they are done. Be sure to pay close attention as they can burn quickly as they contain oil.

Crushing Your Avocado: Halve the avocado, remove the stone, scoop the flesh into a small bowl. Season with a pinch of sea-salt and white pepper, crush with a fork and squeeze in the juice from the other half of the lime.

Assembling to Serve: Divide the citrus fruit salsa into 4 tumblers, evenly spoon the crushed avocado on top, make a final layer with the chilled buckwheat. Sprinkle the toasted pumpkin seeds on top and garnish with some shoot, sprouts or micro leaves if you have them.

Serves: 2 people

BROOKS
— HOTEL —

THE
MAINS

PINEAPPLE CHICKEN CURRY

Trish's Treat – Ann-Marie Donohoe, INTEL

As a mother of 8 children, our Mum Patricia was an avid cook in the kitchen! Like most Irish Mammies, she would have written notes in her cook books "a little at a time" to make sure it had that personal touch! You could never beat coming home to the smell of cooked dinner, especially Mum's Pineapple Chicken Curry – delicious! Sadly our Mum passed away last year, so it's an absolute pleasure to be able to work with ASI and share her recipe, in the hope that many other families will enjoy this loving family recipe – Grubs up!

INGREDIENTS

- 4 chicken breasts
- 4 slices of mango or fresh fruit
- 4tbsp flour
- 1 egg, beaten
- 100g breadcrumbs
- 50g desiccated coconut

For Sauce:

- 55g butter
- 30g curry powder
- 240ml pineapple juice
- 120ml chicken stock
- 120ml cream
- Salt and pepper

METHOD

1. Make a slit at the side of each chicken breast and slip in fruit of choice. Dip in the flour then the egg wash and then a mixture of (desiccated) coconut and bread crumbs. Chill. Either pan fry or roast until golden and cooked through.

SAUCE METHOD:

2. Melt the butter in pan, add the curry powder and cook for 1 minute. Add the pineapple juice, chicken stock and seasoning and simmer for a few minutes to reduce.

3. Add the cream, a little at a time, and reduce to a coating consistency.

4. Whisk in an extra knob of butter (optional).

Serves: 4 people

MAURA'S CHICKEN CURRY

From Maura Dillon, Co. Roscommon

INGREDIENTS

- 6–8 chicken fillets cut into bite size pieces
- 1 tbsp ground coriander
- 1 tbsp ground turmeric
- 1 tbsp ground cumin or ½ tsp cumin seeds
- ½ tsp ground chillies
- 2 oz coconut oil
- 1 tbsp chutney (of your choice)
- 1 tbsp curry paste
- 1 tbsp curry powder
- 1 tin of tomatoes
- 1 tin of coconut milk if desired
- 1 large onion finely chopped
- 2 cloves of garlic finely chopped or grated
- 1 apple cut into small pieces
- 1 piece of ginger finely chopped or grated
- Juice of 1 lemon
- Peppers can also be added if desired

METHOD

1. Fry the onion and garlic in the coconut oil over a medium heat (do not brown).
2. Add the chicken and fry gently for a few minutes.
3. Add all the other ingredients and simmer gently until the chicken is tender – about 20 minutes.
4. Serve with rice of your choice.

Serves: 6 people

SIMON DELANEY'S CHICKEN POT PIE

From Simon Delaney

"The more I understood about the vital work of The Alzheimer Society of Ireland, the more I wanted to help. Dementia should not be ignored or left unspoken. It's affecting our families and friends. And the most important thing we can do is make them feel part of our community. And what better way to feel welcome in someone's life than to cook together? The importance of food and family is very close to my heart."

INGREDIENTS

- 1 tbsp olive oil
- 2 tbsp butter
- 900g boneless skinless chicken thighs, cut into pieces
- 2 medium leeks, washed and chopped into ½-inch pieces
- 2 carrots, roughly chopped
- 3 sticks celery, finely sliced
- 2 tsp dried thyme
- 2½ tbsp flour
- 1 glass white wine
- 1 glass water
- 400ml whole milk
- Salt and pepper
- 180g bacon
- 450g puff pastry
- 1 egg, beaten

✱ Receipe Taken From Simply Simon's The Diner Cookbook

METHOD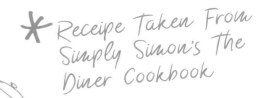

Like most of my one-pot wonders, this starts off by building a base of flavour. In a large casserole pot over a medium heat, add a little olive oil and butter, and when warm, add the chicken, leeks, carrots, celery and the thyme. Cook this for around 15 minutes, then add the flour and continue to stir for a couple of minutes.

Add the glass of wine, followed by a glass of water, and then the milk. Cover the dish with a tight-fitting lid and simmer on the stove for 20 to 30 minutes, until the chicken is tender. Keep an eye on it and stir it every so often so it doesn't stick to the bottom of the pot. The sauce should be loose, but quite thick. If the sauce is a little too loose, continue to cook it with the lid off until it thickens slightly, and if you need to you can add a little more flour. (If you are adding flour, make sure to stir it in so it doesn't go clumpy!) Season the dish with a little salt and freshly ground black pepper.

While this is cooking away, take your rashers and cut them into 2-inch pieces, pop them into a frying pan with a little olive oil, and fry them until nice and crisp.

And so, to assemble the pie. Pour the chicken stew into a large pie dish. Spread the cooked rashers evenly around the top of the stew.

Roll out your pastry, not too thin, to about ¼-inch thick. Egg-wash the rim of the pie dish and drape over the pastry, using a knife to trim the edge of the dish. Egg-wash the top of the pastry to make it go golden while cooking. If you can, crimp the edges of the pastry. You can use the back of your knife to make a nice criss-cross pattern across the top of the pie. This will also allow the pastry to go crisp and flaky. Pop the pie into the centre of your oven and cook for about 30–40 minutes, until golden on top.

Serves: 4–6 people

My research on this dish threw up this fact: the 'pot pie' originated in Greece. Yes, Greece. I had no idea either. The Greeks cooked meats and placed them in open pastry shells that were called Artocreas. And it was the Romans (what have they ever done for us?) who added the top crust making chicken pot pie into an actual pie.

When it comes to the pastry on this pie, I always use the shop-bought puff pastry. If you have the time and the inclination to make the fresh stuff, go for it, I'll admire you from afar. My little twist on the traditional recipe is to add crispy bacon to the pie. Let's go!

CHICKEN WITH TOMATO, BASIL AND MASCARPONE

From Rita Whitcroft, Co. Galway

INGREDIENTS

- 1 skinless chicken crown (750g)
- 500ml fresh chicken stock
- 2 tsp olive oil
- 1 onion, finely chopped
- 2 cloves of garlic, finely chopped
- 2 tbsp tomato purée
- 400g tin chopped tomatoes
- 1 tbsp fresh oregano, chopped
- 2 tbsp basil, chopped, plus extra leaves to garnish
- 2 tsp balsamic vinegar
- 50g reduced-fat mascarpone
- A pinch of dried chilli flakes
- 150g fine green beans, steamed, to serve

METHOD

1. Place the chicken crown, breast side down, in a medium pan and pour the stock and 500ml water. Bring up to a gentle simmer over a medium heat. Cook for 15 minutes, then turn the chicken over and cook for a further 10 minutes, then leave the chicken to cool in the stock.

2. When cool, lift the chicken out of the pan and reserve 200ml of the stock. Using a sharp knife carefully cut the chicken breasts from the bone, keeping them whole.

3. Heat the oil in a frying pan over a medium heat. Add the onion and sauté for 5 minutes to soften, adding a splash of water if it starts to stick. Add the garlic and cook for 2 minutes. Stir in the tomato purée, chopped tomatoes, reserved chicken stock, oregano, some sea salt and freshly ground black pepper. Bring to a simmer and cook for 10 minutes.

4. Add the chopped basil, balsamic vinegar and chicken breasts. Heat through for about 8 minutes. Season the mascarpone with salt, pepper and the chilli flakes, mixing well. Add to the pan and stir to combine with the sauce.

5. Serve with steamed green beans.

Serves: 4 people

CHICKEN WITH TARRAGON

From Gerry Harney, Co. Kildare

INGREDIENTS

Marinade
- 1 tbsp English mustard
- 150ml white wine + extra for sauce
- ½ tsp tarragon
- ½ tsp garlic powder

Sauce
- 170 ml cream
- 1 heaped tsp cornflour
- 1 tbsp brandy
- Salt and pepper to season

- 6 chicken breasts
- 1–2tbsp olive oil or vegetable oil

METHOD

1. Mix the marinade ingredients in a dish and add the chicken breasts. Place in the fridge for 3–4 hours, turning the chicken every 1–2 hours.
2. Preheat the oven to 200°C.
3. Remove the chicken from the marinade and pat dry with kitchen paper. Keep the marinade.
4. Season the chicken with salt and pepper, then fry the chicken in a little oil over a medium heat until browned on both sides. Remove the chicken to a shallow ovenproof dish and set aside.
5. Strain the marinade into the frying pan and add a little extra white wine.
6. Simmer for 5 minutes.
7. Blend the cornflour with the cream in a small bowl or mug and add to the marinade, stirring until thick and smooth.
8. Remove from heat and add the brandy, mixing well.
9. Pour over the chicken and cook in the oven for 10–15 minutes, until the chicken is fully cooked through.
10. Garnish with sprigs of tarragon or parsley.

Serves: 6 people

CHICKEN WITH ASPARAGUS AND PANCETTA

From Anne Gibney, National Office, Dublin

Anne Gibney joined ASI in 2009 and has been a dedicated member of the team ever since. Anne manages the front of house in National Office and always has a kind word and smile to everyone that visits. There is no doubt Mrs G is the boss in National Office, we would be lost without her.

INGREDIENTS

- 2 chicken breasts with skin removed
- Olive oil – for frying
- 3 slices of smoked pancetta
- 8 medium sized asparagus spears, trim the woody ends off.
- 8 cherry tomatoes – halved
- 5–6 black olives with the stones left in
- Small knob of butter
- Handful of basil leaves
- Small bottle of white wine

METHOD

1. Flatten out the chicken with a mallet, keeping it in one piece, but not too thin. (The chicken will cook much faster).

2. Heat the pan and add the oil, brown the chicken on both sides.

3. Place the pancetta on top of the chicken and the asparagus around it: let it cook a little more, then put the pancetta on the bottom of the pan to crisp up and turn the chicken over.

4. Turn up the heat, add the tomatoes, olives, basil and the knob of butter. Remove from the heat and reduce a little more if required.

5. I serve this with small potatoes.

Serves: 2 people

FISH LASAGNE

From Bridie Mc Ginty, Castlebar, Co. Mayo

"I had this meal in London at Antonio Carluccio Restaurant. I asked for the recipe and the young waiter gave it to me when he probably shouldn't have!"

INGREDIENTS

- 8–10 sheets of lasagne
- 25g butter
- 2 cloves garlic crushed
- 40g plain flour
- 240ml dry white wine
- 240ml double cream
- 50g gruyere cheese (grated) or any strong cheese
- 1 bunch spring onions – chopped
- 2 tbsp chopped dill
- 600g–800g mixed fish fillets (salmon, cod, whiting, haddock etc)
- 200g raw peeled tiger prawns
- 1 tbsp oil
- 400g courgette sliced (2 medium courgettes)
- 50g grated parmesan
- Salt and black pepper to taste – sprinkle.
- Optional: Milk to add if more fluid required.

METHOD

1. Pre heat oven to 190°C
2. Melt butter and fry garlic for 30 seconds. Add flour and stir quickly.
3. Add wine gradually and whisk to prevent lumps. Boil for approx. 3 mins to cook flour.
4. Remove from heat. Stir in cream, cheese, spring onions, dill, fish and seafood. Add salt and pepper for seasoning.
5. Put lasagne sheets into large pot of boiling salted water & oil for 8–10 mins.
6. Blanch courgettes for 30 seconds.
7. Put 2–3 sheets of lasagne (enough lasagne sheets to cover) to base of oven proof dish. Spoon in a ⅓ of fish mixture and layer courgettes on top.
8. Repeat layers twice and finish with layer of courgettes. Sprinkle over parmesan and bake for 45 mins or when top is brown and bubbling.
9. Serve with fresh crusty bread and green salad.

Serves: 6 people

SWEET AND SOUR CHICKEN

From Carole Beattie, Co. Cavan

"My husband, Jack, and I moved from Dublin to Cavan along with two of our children and their families. We all wanted a better quality of life, and especially for their young children, away from the huge cost of houses and the hustle and bustle of Dublin. We all bought lovely homes close to one another in an idyllic country setting. Our other daughter had already moved out of Dublin and was living in Mayo.

For two years we enjoyed our rural retreat but sadly after two years I noticed that my husband was showing signs of forgetfulness and in 2006 he was diagnosed with Alzheimer's.

At this point, as a 'blow-in', I didn't know very many people in Cavan outside of my family. So, as Jack continued to deteriorate, I contacted the National Office of The Alzheimer Society of Ireland to see if there was a Support Group available in Cavan. Unfortunately there was not and I received encouragement to start one. The first meeting was attended by three wonderful people who have now become my friends. We have gone from strength to strength, so much so, we were asked to form a branch of which I am Chairperson. I am delighted to say that services in Cavan are now flourishing.

Becoming involved with The Alzheimer Society of Ireland has greatly enriched my life. I've gained lifetime friendships and a huge sense of purpose going forward, despite the loss of my darling husband who sadly passed away in 2012.

My husband Jack was a lovely, gentle soul and we had many humorous moments along his Alzheimers journey. Not least was when he started to forget my name and started thinking that I was his mother. She was a lovely Scottish lady called Dora and she was a great baker. Unfortunately my talents did not come close. His favourites were her sweet and sour chicken, gingerbread and his very special favourite Lemon Pudding.

This sweet and sour chicken recipe was passed down to Dora from her own mother who used it a great deal during the second world war when meat was rationed. I think she adapted it as provisions became scarce but when the whole family moved to Ireland in the fifties, the chicken recipe came too and it was made many times for my husband when he was growing up. They even named it Dora's tasty chicken bake!

I tried as best as I could to replicate her masterpieces, but no matter how hard I tried, I never quite matched up and he told me so! Although he forgot who I was, he never forgot the tastes of his childhood."

INGREDIENTS

- 4 chicken pieces already cooked and skinned
- 227g tin of pineapple in own juice/half medium sized crushed pineapple
- 227g small tin tomatoes
- 85g sugar
- 4 tbsp vinegar
- 3 tbsp soy sauce
- 1½ tbsp corn flour
- 250ml water
- Salt and pepper

METHOD

1. To make sauce: heat sugar, vinegar and soy sauce together in pan.
2. Mix the corn flour gradually with a little of the water and pour into pan – stir well until mixture thickens, simmer for 5 mins.
3. Add pineapple, tomatoes and season well.
4. Add chicken pieces and cook over a low heat until very hot.

Serves: 4 people

SPICE PORK WITH TOMATO SAUCE

From Raymond Cregan , Co. Dublin

Ray is a member of The Dementia Carers' Campaign Network. The Alzheimer Society of Ireland facilitates and supports the network, an advocacy group for those who have experienced caring for a loved one with dementia. It aims to represent, raise awareness and campaign on the distinct needs of people who care for someone with dementia.

INGREDIENTS

- 2 Pork tenderloins, trimmed of fat and sinew

For the marinade:
- 2 tbsp olive oil
- 1 tsp ground cumin
- 1 tsp ground coriander
- 1 tsp hot smoked paprika
- 2 cloves of garlic, peeled and crushed
- Finely grated zest of 1 lemon
- Leaves from a few springs of thyme
- Sea salt and freshly ground black pepper

For the tomato sauce:
- 120ml extra virgin olive oil
- 2 small onions finely chopped
- I carton of passata
- 1 bay leaf
- 1 tsp unrefined light brown sugar
- Sea salt and freshly ground black pepper

METHOD

1. To make the marinade, mix all the ingredients in a bowl, add the pork and cover and chill for 1–4 hours.

2. For the sauce, heat the oil in a medium sauce-pan, add the chopped onions and season with salt and pepper. Cook over a low heat for 20 minutes until the onions are soft.

3. Add the passata and bay leaf to the onions and cook for another 20 minutes until the sauce is thick. Season with salt and pepper and add paprika and some sugar to sweeten to taste.

4. While the sauce is cooking, drain the pork of the marinade and pan-fry until browned and seared on all sides. Place on a baking tray and cook at 180°C for 12–15 minutes until cooked through (check by inserting a sharp knife to the centre of the tenderloin and holding it there for 3 seconds. Touch the tip of the knife to the inside of your wrist; if it's hot to the touch, it's cooked through.)

5. Serve with boiled rice and asparagus.

Serves: 4–6 people

NANNY RITA'S STEW

From Lisa Marie O'Reily, Dublin

"This dish reminds me of my childhood although it may have been adapted slightly over the years. Once the weather got bad my nanny Rita would get the big pot out and make her famous stew. Try as I might, I've never quite replicated the flavour but it's an adaptable dish and simple enough for anyone to make. The ingredients can be altered to suit your personal taste. I am honoured to have been asked to add a recipe for the Alzheimer's Society cookbook. I have been a volunteer here in Dublin for a number of years after my dad was diagnosed with vascular dementia. Recently my mam has also been diagnosed with Alzheimer's so I have begun to support and give back as much of my time to the society as possible as they do amazing work supporting families like mine. I hope that this recipe can put a smile on someone's face, and above all, inspire memories."

INGREDIENTS

- 1 bag of baby potatoes, if preferred you can use large potatoes or even sweet potato
- 2–3 carrots
- 1 large onion
- 1 small turnip
- 2–3 parsnips
- 1 leek

- 500–600g minced beef
- Oxtail soup – 1 large family pack
- Beef & vegetable soup – 1 large family pack
- Beef or vegetable stock pot – 1 or 2 depending on taste
- 50 g of flour
- ½ tsp of salt & ½ tsp of pepper

METHOD

1. Peel & chop all the veg ingredients, I normally chop them into small-medium square cubed pieces as I find they cook better. If preferred you can leave the baby potatoes whole.

2. Get a large pot & put veg in, put enough cold water in the pot to cover the veg & put on a low heat.

3. With the soup I make up a thick soup in a bowl to make sure I have broken down the granules so there's no lumps, you can use a hand whisk if you want. I find the back of a spoon works really well. Once smooth then add to the pot. Stir pot occasionally on a low heat. **Important – taste as you go, you might need to add salt or pepper.

4. In another large bowl, mix mince, flour, salt & pepper. Once mixed take small amounts of the mixture & roll into small meatballs. Once done then spray fry lite or use a little vegetable oil in a frying pan. Slowly fry the meatballs until brown. Once done add to the stew pot.

5. Taste stew, you may want to add another flavour or more salt & pepper. This is personal taste. If you find it too salty you can add a small amount of tomato puree if you have that to hand to tone down the salt flavour.

6. Adjust heat to medium, stir until it starts to boil or bubble around the sides of the pot. Then turn down to a low heat & let it cook away. Stir occasionally and check veg pieces as you are going along, add the stock pot half way through cooking.

7. Leave to cook for about an hour so all the flavours combine.

8. When cooked you can serve up in small bowls with some fresh crusty bread. If you prefer it to be smoother then pop some into a blender.

Serves: 6–8 people

KIDNEY TURBIGO

From Kitty Quinn, Co. Mayo

"Originally, Kitty was incapable of boiling an egg. But after she married Maurice in 1955, her mother-in-law gifted her a book entitled 'The Right Way To His Heart'. This was a stroke of good fortune for Maurice – his appetite was shaped as a hungry teenager during WWII rationing in Dublin city and he simply loved food. Taking this 'subtle' advice earnestly, Kitty attended a series of Cordon Bleu cookery classes, after which she would type up the recipes and add handwritten notes as she began to perfect the methods. And so began 60 years of happy marriage with fine dining at the heart of both their social and personal lives.

Every week, for 50 years Kitty prepared Maurice his favourite dish: Kidneys Turbigo. While the rest of us groaned and bemoaned the foul smell of kidney permeating the entire house, Maurice would grin, make sucking noises and smack his lips together in anticipation as the lid was lifted off the saute pan in front of him...every time.

Dementia chipped away at, and eventually completely eliminated, Kitty's capacity, desire and willingness to cook. As Maurice was himself an excellent cook, he eventually, seamlessly took sole responsibility for their food preparation for the last ten years of their marriage, until his death. He never prepared Kidneys Turbigo."

INGREDIENTS

- 5 lamb kidneys
- 12–18 pickling onions
- 55g butter
- 110g chipolata sausages
- 110g button mushrooms (quartered)
- 2tsp flour
- 1 tsp tomato puree
- 1 tbsp sherry
- 215ml brown stock (beef)
- Salt and pepper
- 1 bay leaf
- 2 slices of stale bread (cut into croutes)
- Oil (for frying croutes) parsley (chopped)

METHOD

1. Blanch the onions and drain. Skin the kidneys, cut in half lengthways and core. Heat a saute or deep frying pan, drop in the butter and, when it is foaming, put in the kidneys and saute briskly until evenly browned.

2. Lift out kidneys and put in chipolata sausages, lower the heat and cook over a brisk heat for 2–3 mins, then draw pan aside. Stir in the flour, tomato puree, sherry and stock and bring to the boil, add the bayleaf and season. Slice sausages and kidneys and put in the pan. Cover and simmer gently for 20–25 mins (1 hour if using pork kidneys) or until tender. Serve the kidneys and sausages surrounded with croutes, and sprinkle with parsley.

3. For croutes, cut bread into triangular pieces and fry in a little hot oil until golden brown. Bon appetite!

Serves: 2 people

ORANGE STUFFING

From Maeve Montgomery, Dementia Adviser in Cavan/Monaghan/Louth

"This is a recipe for stuffing to accompany roast chicken. Years ago, when I was living in Dublin I met someone who used to add freshly-squeezed orange to their stuffing for chicken. I told my mother about it and we tried it out. She decided to also add the grated rind of the orange – and it was even tastier. I discovered that you could replace the fat in the stuffing with the orange juice if you added the juice of the whole orange, making it a healthier option."

Maeve started working with The Alzheimer Society of Ireland in September 2002 as a Home Care Co-ordinator in County Louth and worked with families in the community providing care to people with dementia in their own home. Maeve was appointed a Dementia Adviser in 2014 with responsibility for the Cavan/Monaghan/Louth regions. 16 years of great service.

"I am one of eight Dementia Advisers with The Alzheimer Society of Ireland who work nationwide with people living with dementia, their families and carers to provide a highly responsive and individualised information and signposting service. Our aim is to help people live well with dementia and to help people understand dementia and brain health."

The Dementia Adviser's role is to support people as soon as possible after diagnosis and stay with them as they progress though the dementia journey.

Your local Dementia Adviser will work with you to:

- provide information and advice throughout your journey with dementia,

- help connect you with dementia supports and services,

- help connect you with local groups and services, and

- help your community to be more dementia friendly.

This service is free and confidential

Call 1800 341 341 or visit alzheimer.ie to find out more about this service.

INGREDIENTS

- I put half of the onions into the cavity of the chicken.
- Put chicken into the oven roast
- I make the stuffing: Onion, breadcrumbs, salt, pepper, parsley, thyme, the grated peel of an orange, the freshly squeezed juice of the orange.
- Form the stuffing into sausage shapes and wrap it in rashers of bacon.
- Then smear the bacon with mustard and roll it into brown sugar.
- Place on a lightly oiled oven proof dish.
- This is then cooked separately it can be put into the oven approx. 20 mins before the chicken is ready.

METHOD

1. The result is a delicious accompaniment to a roast chicken.

2. We often made this together for Sunday lunch when I was home at the weekend before I was married. It is a rare and treasured memory of me teaching my mother a recipe, but of course she was able to improve it.

GOBBY'S MEDITERRANEAN ROASTED VEGETABLE FETA TART

From Davina Smith, Co. Cork

"My mum would whip this up in a flash and, in earnest, no recipe was followed – it all came from her memory and her wonderful culinary instinct. Ingredients would change as the seasons changed with butternut squash a favourite in the autumn. Plus, for meat lovers, ham or cooked meats were added. 'Is the veggie tart on?' would often be asked as family and friends entered the house but the smell of it would answer their question. It was also great served cold for brekkie/lunch/snacks too! Gets the WOW factor every time."

INGREDIENTS

- 2 courgettes, halved lengthways, cut into 2cm pieces
- 1 red pepper, deseeded and roughly/thickly chopped
- 2 red onions, cut into chunky wedges
- 1 medium aubergine, sliced and chopped
- 10 cherry tomatoes
- 2 tbsp. olive oil plus extra for drizzling
- 320g/12oz sheet ready-rolled puff

- pastry 200g/7oz feta crumbled
- 4 tbsp of sun dried tomato paste
- 1 free-range egg, beaten
- 2 tsp fresh thyme leaves
- Salt and freshly ground black pepper
- Flour for dusting pastry
- Mixed salad leaves and dressing to serve

METHOD

1. Preheat oven to gas mark 6/200°C (180°C in a fan oven).
2. Add courgettes, aubergine, peppers and onion into a roasting tin.
3. Drizzle with oil, Season with salt and pepper and mix to coat all the vegetables in the 1 tbsp of the oil.
4. Roast in the oven for 10 minutes, or until the vegetables are just starting to go tender – Don't overcook at this stage.
5. Set aside to cool slightly.
6. Lay the ready-rolled sheet of puff pastry onto a lightly floured/lined baking tray and create a border and lightly brush the border edge with beaten egg.
7. Using a fork, pierce pastry base a number of times but don't pierce all the way through.
8. Put pastry in oven for about 12–15 mins until pale golden. If it puffs up, it's ok as you can gently push it down with a wooden spoon.
9. Spread tomato paste across pastry base (not the border as may burn) and remaining oil. Within the border scatter the roasted vegetable, tomatoes and crumble over feta. Top with thyme leaves and a sprinkle of freshly ground black pepper.
10. Put back in oven for a further 10–15 mins, or until veg is tender and feta has melted and the pastry is crisp and golden-brown and a crispy bottom!
11. Drizzle with a little more oil to serve if you wish.
12. Serve with dressed mixed salad leaves and enjoy.

Serves: 4–6 people

SHEPHERD'S PIE

Phyllis O'Rourke, Cairdeas, Co. Dublin

"This particular recipe was usually Thursday's dinner because you would be waiting for the wages on Friday. It was called 'waiting day'."

INGREDIENTS

- 450g minced beef or lamb
- 1 large onion
- 30g plain flour
- 240ml stock
- Salt and pepper
- 1kg creamed potatoes
- Gravy browning

METHOD

1. Preheat oven to 180°C.
2. Fry the meat and set aside on a plate, removing surplus fat. Melt some of the dripping and fry the onions.
3. Stir in the flour, add the gravy browning and meat.
4. Mix well and turn into the dish.
5. Pile the creamed potatoes on top on the meat.
6. Cook in the oven for 40 minutes.

Serves: 4 people

EDDIE'S DUBLIN CODDLE

Eddie Winterlich, Co. Meath

"This recipe came from the 2nd World War when food was scarce. It was a poor man's stew. Whatever was available in the house went into this stew."

INGREDIENTS

- 225g sausages
- 225g rashers
- 1 onion chopped
- 2 cloves of garlic crushed
- 2 sticks of celery
- 3 potatoes quartered
- 1 vegetable stock cube
- 1 tablespoon of barley
- Enough water to cover ingredients

METHOD

1. Put all ingredients into a pot and cover with water. Bring to the boil and put on a low heat & simmer for 2 hours

Serves: 4 people

FINNAN HADDOCK AU GRATIN

Maire Gorman, Co. Dublin

"My Mam Nora was born in Mitchelstown Co. Cork. There was no secondary school for girls in Mitchelstown at that time. So, at 11 years of age, she moved to Dublin and went to boarding school in Loreto on the Green with her sisters and cousins. There were two boarding schools, a Gaelscoil and an English school. Nora attended the Gaelscoil.

Food was scarce during the war but she always recalled they had 'fish and confessions on Fridays' as was the norm for Catholics at the time. She loves fish but had never had fresh fish until she came to Dublin as it was unavailable in Mitchelstown up to the 1960's – it was so far from the sea.

Nora was a stay-at-home mother who taught me how to cook and knit and sew. She often cooked quite complicated dishes like deep fried sweet and sour pork and stuffed beef olives. There was always fresh fruit and vegetables in season for dinner courtesy of Nora's husband Donal who was an avid gardener.

Nora is a very cheerful person and always has a smile on her face. She is very contented and never gets angry or complains. She has always been like this. She never got angry with us as children. She loved swimming and brought us to the nearby beaches at Sutton and Dollymount whenever the sun shone. Her disposition and love of good food is the secret of her long life. 'Ní bheidh a leithéad ann arís!'.

Nora has been a client of Cairdeas Day Care in Raheny for 15 years. She is one of their longest attending clients and loves attending Cairdeas. The staff there are amazing. They are always in great form which makes it really pleasant for those attending and gives family the peace of mind that their loved ones are being cared for. Mam has really benefited from Cairdeas. It also gives us, her carers, a break to recharge our batteries."

INGREDIENTS

- 680g smoked haddock
- 120ml water
- 2 hardboiled eggs
- Bouquet garni
- 240ml milk
- 1 chopped onion

- SAUCE:
- 30g Flour
- 350ml liquid in which fish has been cooked
- 30g butter

- TOPPING:
- 85g grated cheese
- 15g butter
- 30g breadcrumbs

METHOD

1. Steep fish in boiling water for 2 mins. Remove skin and fins and break into large chunks.

2. Put into saucepan with milk and water and bouquet garni. Bring slowly to the boil and simmer for about 10 mins till tender.

3. Lift fish out and break into pieces. Put into greased Pyrex dish with ½ cheese over it.

4. Melt butter, sauté onion gently, mix in flour. Cook for 3 mins, add liquid. Cook for 7 mins stirring continuously.

5. Pour sauce over fish in dish. Sprinkle with rest of cheese and breadcrumbs and chopped hard boiled eggs. Place a few pieces of butter on top.

6. Bake in oven at 180°C until hot and light brown.

Serves: 6 people

BAKED SALMON WITH ALMOND AND PESTO CRUST

Sabina Brennan, PhD., C.PsSl.
Trinity Brain Health and ADAPT,
Trinity College Dublin.

Sabina Brennan has been involved with The Alzheimer Society of Ireland since 2010. She has collaborated with ASI on a number of important research and intervention projects especially on areas like cognitive rehabilitation, early intervention and carer well-being. Sabina serves on the ASI Advocacy committee. She is also a member of The Alzheimer Society Medical and Scientific Advisory Panel.

"I had developed several animations and websites to address people's fears around memory loss and dementia, to offer practical advice and to promote brain health. Around that time, my own mum became very ill and went on to develop dementia. One of my dearest memories is attending an ASI event – my mum was in a nursing home at that point and was delighted to be out at the event. She wore her favourite dress and had a fantastic time. Tina Leonard shared some professional photographs taken at the event of myself with my mum. They are so dear and special to me as she was so happy that evening.

This recipe has many fond memories. I served it to the RTÉ String Quartet when they rehearsed in my house (how lucky am I? – my son is a classical saxophonist and they were preforming together). I also served it when the Head of Amnesty International, Colm O'Gorman, came to dinner in our house before speaking at an event for Marriage Equality – I spoke at their launch in 2015.

This dish uses ground almonds rather than processed breadcrumbs for the crust. You can make your own pesto or use a store-bought pesto but make sure you buy one made with fresh ingredients and no preservatives. Salmon is a nutritious brain food because it is packed with omega-3 fatty acids, which keep your brain running smoothly. Almonds are a fantastic source of anti-oxidants, which help to protect against oxidative stress, which is not good for the health of your brain.

My mum loved salmon, however, I can't recall whether she ever ate this particular dish at my house – in her last few years she had trouble swallowing so when we took her home from the nursing home at weekends she always asked for Cully and Sully's tomato soup – it was her favourite and so we gave it to her every time."

METHOD

INGREDIENTS

- 2 salmon fillet steak portions (Supreme)
- 2 tbsp (level) of finely ground almonds
- 2 tbsp (level) of fresh pesto
- 1 tbsp (level) of freshly grated Parmesan cheese
- Juice of ½ a lemon
- A small amount of coconut oil for the baking tray
- Black pepper to season.

1. Pre-heat your oven to 230°C. Cover a baking tray (25x35cm approx.) with tinfoil. Lightly oil the tinfoil with coconut oil.

Prep your fish:

2. Run your hand gently along the surface of the fish and remove any stray bones that may have been missed during filleting. Leave the skin on your fish.

3. Place the two salmon fillets on the oiled tray, skin-side down. Squeeze lemon juice over both fillets. Lightly season with pepper.

The Crust:

1. Place all of the pesto in a bowl and give it a good stir to mix it well.

Add ⅓ of the ground almonds to the pesto and mix well to form a good paste. Spread this mixture evenly over the two salmon fillets.

2. Mix half the parmesan with the remaining ground almonds and place over the two fillets on top of the pesto-almond paste.

3. Scatter the remaining parmesan on top of each fillet. Place on the middle shelf in the oven and cook for 10 minutes. This will give a crispy crust and moist salmon fillet.

4. This dish is equally delicious served with a colourful Mediterranean salad or with broccoli and fine beans, all of which are great for brain health.

Serves: 2 people

THE MURROUGH POSH FISH PIE

From Catherine Fulvio, Co. Wicklow

This was my mother's signature fish dish. We traipsed around the whole island of Ireland with this dish as she entered fish-cookery competitions across the country. She used to present the pie in scallop shells and as kids we used to think, 'How posh!' Now I think, 'How very 1980s!'

INGREDIENTS

For the filling:
- 300ml milk
- 2 bay leaves
- 3 tbsp butter
- 4 tbsp plain flour
- Salt and freshly ground black pepper
- 2 tsp chopped parsley
- 2 tsp roughly chopped chervil
- 150g smoked haddock, diced
- 150g salmon, diced
- 200g skinless white fish such as haddock, cod or pollack, diced
- 150g prawns, shelled

For the mashed potatoes;
- 4 large potatoes, steamed
- 30g butter
- 100ml milk
- Pinch of nutmeg
- Salt and freshly ground black pepper

For the mashed sweet potato;
- 1 medium sweet potato, steamed
- 2 to 3 tbsp milk
- 1 tbsp butter
- Salt and freshly ground black pepper

METHOD

1. Preheat the oven to 180°C/fan 160°C/gas 4. Brush a medium-sized gratin dish with melted butter.

2. To prepare the filling, pour the milk into a medium saucepan over a medium heat with the bay leaves, butter and flour and stir until a thick sauce forms. Season with salt and freshly ground black pepper and add the chopped parsley and chervil. Add the diced fish and prawns to the sauce and simmer gently until the fish is just cooked. This should take about 5 minutes. Check the seasoning again.

3. To prepare the potatoes, push the warm potatoes through a ricer. Warm the milk and butter in the microwave and add to the potatoes with a little grated nutmeg, salt and pepper. Spoon into a piping bag with a star nozzle. Now mash the sweet potatoes and add the milk, butter, salt and pepper. Spoon into another piping bag with another star nozzle.

4. To assemble, spoon the fish into the gratin dish. Pipe a line of sweet potato diagonally across and then pipe the potato over the rest of the pie. Place in the oven for about 12 to 15 minutes until the top is lightly golden. Serve with a green salad.

Serves: 4 people

EATING WELL WITH DEMENTIA

Good nutrition is essential for health and well-being. For people living with dementia, getting the correct nutrition through food can sometimes be difficult. It is important to remember that dementia can affect each person differently. As dementia progresses, changes may develop that can impact eating and drinking. This can lead to under-eating resulting in weight loss, or over-eating, causing weight gain.

It can be upsetting to see someone we care about struggle with eating and drinking and to see weight loss or weight gain. Good practical nutritional advice can help people with dementia manage these challenges and remain strong, healthy and independent for as long as possible.

Eating a healthy, balanced diet is essential to maintain good health for everyone. Choosing a variety of foods from different food groups can help achieve this balance, and ensure that the body gets all the nutrients that it needs to stay well.

Here are some hints and tips to encourage good eating habits and help the person with dementia be as independent as possible during meals:

Keep the table setting simple
A relaxed and calm environment will help the person with dementia to focus on what they are eating, so avoid too much clutter on the table. Keep condiments and sauces to a minimum.

Establish a routine around eating and meal times that works well for everyone
Use prompts to signal that it is time to eat. This could be involving the person with dementia in meal preparation or in setting the table or it could be a prompt such as eating lunch when the news is on.

Company at mealtimes can make them more sociable and enjoyable.
Eating with others can encourage a person with dementia to eat, and they can copy actions if a prompt is needed.

THE ALZHEIMER SOCIETY *of* IRELAND

Think colour and contrast

Contrasting colours will help identify foods, so use plain plates and cups which are in contrast to the table and therefore stand out. Avoid patterned table cloths and plates. Make food attractive by trying a variety of different colours and shapes – it's important to be tempted by the food that we see.

Familiarity is important

Having the table set in a familiar way helps. A favourite plate or cup may act as a prompt. Is there a preferred seat at the table? Where possible, stick to established meal patterns according to the individual's established preference.

Be flexible around food choices

People with dementia can sometimes become confused about which items 'go together'. They may mix dessert with main courses or add drinks to a main meal. There is no harm done especially if the food is still eaten.

Allow sufficient time

It may take longer for the person with dementia to finish a meal, so allow sufficient time. Avoid having too much food on a plate at any time, and allow time between courses. Use of plate warmers and insulated cups will help to keep food and drinks warm. Try not to clear plates away until everyone seated at the table is finished, as removing plates can be a signal to stop eating.

Little and often

As people get older, they often prefer to eat smaller meals, more frequently. Instead of three main meals a day, try five or six small snacks distributed throughout the day.

Be flexible to food preferences

Develop a food preference list and remember to adjust as tastes change. Try not to exclude foods too quickly and re-try ones that haven't been tried for a while.

Don't worry about neatness

If the person with dementia is struggling with cutlery, this may result in some spills and mess around the table. Try using non-stick mats or plates with suction cups and a wipe-clean table cloth to make cleaning up easier. Encourage the person to feed themselves as much as possible.

Use finger foods

Try including finger foods that can be easily eaten without cutlery. These are ideal for those who have difficulty using cutlery or are restless and like to walk around at mealtimes.

Information taken from Eating well with dementia: practical tips for family carers available online at www.alzheimer.ie.
For more information on this topic please contact our national helpline on 1800 341 341

THE DESSERTS

PINEAPPLE FRUIT CAKE

From Gerry Gaffney, Co. Cavan

This is a famous recipe of my mum's. I grew up eating this everyday as my mother made two daily and it was put on the table at each sitting.

INGREDIENTS

- 170g butter
- 225g dark brown sugar
- 425g pineapple chunks, diced
- 225g sultanas
- 225g raisins
- 285g self-raising flour
- 1 tsp baking soda
- ½ tsp cinnamon
- ½ tsp ground ginger
- ½ tsp mixed spice
- Pinch of salt
- 3 eggs

METHOD

1. Preheat oven to 180°C and grease a 20cm square tin.
2. Melt the butter, add the sugar, pineapple and 4 tablespoons juice and the dried fruit, and bring to the boil. Simmer for 5 mins and set aside to cool.
3. Beat the eggs and stir into the cooled mixture, then add the flour and spices
4. Mix well and pour into the tin.
5. Bake for 1 hr 15 mins at 180°C.

Serves: 6–8 people

COURGETTE CAKE

From Margaret Barker, Co. Sligo

Margaret Barker was one of the founding members of the Sligo Branch of ASI. She volunteered tirelessly for many years in the Dunally Day Care Centre. Margaret was involved in fundraising and other activities with service users. She created the beautiful gardens at Dunally Day Care Centre. Margaret baked this wonderful cake on several occasions for service users.

INGREDIENTS

- 2 large eggs
- 85g soft brown sugar
- 1 tsp vanilla extract
- 2 tsp cinnamon
- ½ tsp bicarb soda
- 85g walnuts roughly chopped
- 125ml vegetable oil
- 350g courgette coarsely grated
- 300g plain flour
- ¼ tsp nutmeg
- ½ tsp baking powder
- 140g sultanas (optional)

METHOD

1. Heat oven to 180°C and line a 1kg/2lb loaf tin with greaseproof paper.

2. In a large bowl, whisk the eggs, oil and sugar then add the courgettes and vanilla.

3. In another bowl combine the remaining ingredients with a pinch of salt.

4. Stir the dry ingredients into the wet mixture and then pour into the tin.

5. Bake for 60–75 mins or until a skewer inserted into the centre comes out clean.

6. Leave to cool. Can be frozen for up to one month.

Serves: 8 people

FRENCH PANCAKES

From Geraldine McDonnell, Bagenalstown, Co. Carlow

This recipe originates from "Mrs Beaton's Book of Household Management", left to me by my son-in-law!

INGREDIENTS

- 2 eggs
- 50g butter
- 50g sugar
- 50g flour
- Milk as needed

METHOD

1. Put eggs and butter into a basin, beat into a creamy texture.

2. Stir in the sugar and flour mixing well adding milk in turns as needed.

3. Mix both combinations above and keep stirring/beating for a few minutes.

4. Put the mix on buttered plates and bake in hot oven for 20 minutes or until cooked.

5. Serve pancakes with lemon and sugar or pile pancakes on a dish with a layer of preserve or marmalade in between each pancake.

Serves: 4–6 people, can be served any time of the year

APPLE DUMPLINGS

From Mary Bolger, Co. Kildare

My husband's aunt who had dementia made this for me when I was invited to tea 40 years ago. I will remember forever the first time I tasted this.

Aunt Kay was a great cook and she made this on a regular basis. The smell of cooking apples and cinnamon all through the house and rich custard with cinnamon. Scrumptious.

INGREDIENTS

- 9 tbsp of sugar
- 3½ tsp baking powder
- ½ tsp salt
- 60ml milk
- 2 tbsp suet
- 3 large apples
- 1 tbsp ground cinnamon
- 1–2 tbsp brown sugar
- 225g plain flour

METHOD

1. Sift together 3 tbsp of sugar, baking powder, salt, flour, and the suet and add the milk. On a floured board, roll out the dough to about ½ cm thick and cut the dough into 15cm squares.

2. Peel and halve the apples and core them. Put half an apple onto each piece of dough. Place a teaspoon of sugar and a pinch of cinnamon onto the top of each apple.

3. Pull the corners of the each dough square to wrap up the apple half and close them together, press and seal well.

4. Tie each dumpling into a piece of cheesecloth or muslin.

5. Drop the dumplings into a large pot of boiling water.

6. Cook for about 25 mins, remove to a large plate and remove the muslin. Pierce with a sharp knife to check that the apples are cooked through.

7. Preheat grill.

8. Place the cooked dumplings onto an oven proof dish and sprinkle them with cinnamon powder and a pinch of brown sugar and grill for 5–10 mins.

9. Serve with thick creamy cinnamon custard.

Serves: 3–6 people

COUNTRY RHUBARB CAKE

Darina Allen, Ballymaloe Cookery School, Co. Cork

"This traditional rhubarb cake, based on an enriched bread dough, was made all over Ireland and is a treasured memory from my childhood. It would have originally been baked in the bastible or 'baker' over the open fire. My mother, who taught me this recipe, varied the filling with the seasons – first rhubarb, then gooseberries, later in the autumn, apples and plums. The Country Rhubarb Cake may or will hopefully trigger nostalgic memories of childhood for many."

INGREDIENTS

- 350g (12oz) plain flour, plus extra for dusting
- pinch of salt
- ½ teaspoon bread soda (bicarbonate of soda)
- 50g (2oz) caster sugar
- 75g (3oz) butter
- 1 egg, free-range if possible
- 165ml (5½fl oz) milk, buttermilk or sour milk
- 680g (1½lb) rhubarb, finely chopped
- 175–225g (6–8oz) granulated sugar
- beaten egg, to glaze
- caster sugar, for sprinkling

METHOD

1. Preheat the oven to 180°C/350ºF/Gas Mark 4

2. Sieve the flour, salt, bicarbonate of soda and caster sugar into a bowl and rub in the butter. Whisk the egg and mix with the milk, buttermilk or sour milk. Make a well in the centre of the dry ingredients. Pour in most of the liquid and mix to a soft dough; add the remainder of the liquid if necessary.

3. Sprinkle a little flour on the work surface. Turn out the soft dough and pat gently into a round. Divide into two pieces: one should be slightly larger than the other; keep the larger one for the lid.

4. Dip your fingers in flour. Roll out the smaller piece of pastry to fit the pie plate. Scatter the finely chopped rhubarb all over the base and sprinkle with granulated sugar. Brush the edges of the pastry with beaten egg. Roll out the other piece of dough until it is exactly the right size to cover the plate, lift it on and press the edges gently to seal them. Make a hole in the centre for the steam to escape. Brush again with beaten egg and sprinkle with a very small amount of caster sugar.

5. Bake in the oven for 45 minutes to 1 hour or until the rhubarb is soft and the crust is golden. Leave it to sit for 15–20 minutes before serving so that the juice can soak into the crust. Sprinkle with caster sugar. Serve still warm, with a bowl of softly whipped cream and some moist, brown sugar.

Serves: 6–8 people

CHESTER CAKE

From Johanna Lynch, Co. Tipperary

On one of our Tea Days at Waterman's Lodge, I was talking to an elderly gentleman who has since passed away and we were talking about different cakes that we liked. The one that stood out for me from our chat was Chester Cake. He said he remembered as a child being given a few bob and sent to the local bakery to get a big chunk of it and it would fill you for the day. He said the bakery would make it at the weekend with all the stale ends of bread and cakes. After the Tea Day I made it for our clients and it gave me great pleasure when some of them remembered it.

INGREDIENTS

- 340g stale bread
- 1 small pot of tea
- 110g plain flour
- 2 tbsp mixed spice
- 1 tsp baking powder
- 255g brown sugar
- 55g butter
- 255g sultanas
- 2 eggs
- 120ml milk

Shortcrust Pastry:
- 340g plain flour
- 170g butter or margarine
- Water

Icing:
- 200g icing sugar
- 2–3 tbsp lemon juice

METHOD

1. Cover the stale bread with the cold tea. Leave to soak for 1 hour.

2. Preheat the oven to 180°C. Butter a rectangular (20.5 cm x 32 cm) baking tin.

3. Squeeze the bread dry by pressing the mixture in a sieve over the sink. Transfer to a bowl and set aside.

4. Sieve the flour, mixed spice and baking powder into a bowl, then add the sugar. Rub in the butter with your fingertips until the mixture resembles breadcrumbs.

5. Add the sultanas to the bread and mix well, then add to the flour mixture and combine well.

6. Beat the eggs with the milk in a jug. Add to the bread and flour and mix well.

7. Roll one half of the pastry to fit into the buttered baking tin. Prick the pastry base all over with a fork.

8. Spread the bread mixture over the pastry. Roll out the other half of the pastry, then cover the bread mixture with it and pinch the edges together to seal. Prick the top with a fork. Bake for 1 hour 45 minutes, until golden. Cover loosely with foil if the pastry is browning too much. Leave to cool on a rack.

9. To make the icing, mix the lemon juice with the sugar until thick. Add more icing sugar or water depending on how thick the icing is.

10. Spread generously over the cake and slice once set.

Serves: 14–16 people

BAILEY'S BALLS

From Eilis Bailey, Co. Galway

I made these for the ICA ladies and they got a great laugh at the name but they all wanted a copy of the recipe which is very simple to make.

INGREDIENTS

- 300g chocolate coated biscuits
- 250g mascarpone cheese
- 80ml Bailey's Irish Cream
- 300g white chocolate roughly chopped
- 2–4 squares milk chocolate

METHOD

1. Crush biscuits to make crumbs.
2. Add cream cheese and baileys and mix thoroughly.
3. Make into approx. 20 balls. Rest in fridge for 45 mins.
4. When balls are chilled melt white chocolate and coat balls in it and return to fridge to chill.
5. Melt milk chocolate and drizzle over balls from teaspoon.

Serves: 10 people

HEALTHY BROWNIE AND CHOCOLATE GANACHE

Jeeny Maltese, Co. Galway

'Cooking is such an important part of everyday life. And I believe it should be fun and easy to do. Little everyday tasks are so important to people's independence too. I hope my brownie recipe helps someone have fun in the kitchen and regain a little spirit too. I'm honoured to be part of this book and delighted to support the tireless work of The Alzheimer Society of Ireland."

INGREDIENTS

Brownie
- 2½ cups ground almonds
- ½ cup unsweetened cocoa powder
- 1½ cups pitted dates
- 1½ tsp baking powder
- 1 tsp bread soda
- Pinch sea salt
- 1 cup boiling water
- 3 whole eggs (or 3 chia eggs for vegans)
- 2 tbsp coconut oil
- 2 tsp vanilla extract
- (Optional: 2 tbsp maple syrup)

Ganache
- 4 tbsp cocoa powder
- 2 tbsp coconut oil
- 4 tbsp coconut milk or any milk
- 2 tbsp maple syrup
- 2 tsp vanilla

METHOD

1. Just mix in a bowl all your dry ingredients with a whisk, ground almonds, cocoa powder, baking powder, bread soda and sea salt, mix well and set aside.
2. Blend with a hand blender all your wet ingredients together, dates, boiling water, vanilla, maple syrup and eggs. (While hot).
3. Mix together all wet and dry ingredients until well combined. Do not over mix.
4. Bake in a Brownie tin lined with greaseproof paper at 160°C Gas Mark 3 for 35–45 minutes. Let cool before decorating.

Ganache

Just melt gently together all ingredients, coconut oil, cocoa powder, coconut milk, maple syrup and vanilla. Mix well with a whisk, allow to cool slightly and decorate your brownie. Or you could just melt dark chocolate with coconut milk & maple syrup.

Serves: 12 people

Nutrition Tips: We all should include more greens, berries, nuts, seeds and vegetables in our daily diets. Here are "brain healthy" food groups that help protect against Alzheimer's: green leafy vegetables, other vegetables, nuts, berries, beans, whole grains, green tea, turmeric, ginger, cinnamon, rosemary, garlic, etc. Here are the food groups you should avoid: Trans fats, processed foods, gluten, margarine, processed dairy products. These foods cause inflammation and circulation problems, restricting blood flow to the brain.

BANANA ICE CREAM

From Declan Cassidy, Co. Louth

"Along with my siblings we were dividing the week to take turns caring for my mother, Jo Cassidy. Mum loves ice-cream lollies. As she became difficult to deal with, ice creams became a way to appease her. The doctor had said that getting any food into her was positive so it reached a stage where she could well have been having three or four ice-creams a day. Her clothes began to get tight and we were worried about the health implications. Recently Mum began to make strange with my siblings but not with me so I am now looking after her full time. I've used the opportunity of having her around the clock to regulate her diet. Mum enjoys bananas and a German friend of mine gave me a simple recipe which has banished the ice-cream to an occasional Sunday Treat. Mum now eats homemade banana 'ice-creams/pops'

INGREDIENTS

- 3 bananas
- 60–120ml milk

METHOD

1. Mush the bananas in a bowl with a fork or similar utensil (I get Mum to do this).
2. Add milk and mix well until a smooth consistency is achieved. Pour mixture into ice pop moulds (I got a box of six in Heatons) Freeze.
3. I dip the mould into a cup of hot water to release the ice-creams smoothly. The mixture can be frozen in a tub instead if you want to make ice-cream to scoop. Coconut or almond milk can be used instead of cow's milk for a vegan version (though this will be more icy) or for an even thicker ice-cream, leave out the milk altogether.

Serves: 6 people

CHOCOLATE BROWNIES

From Kaye Cullen, Co. Tipperary

A family favourite for all birthdays and special occasions in the Cullen household over the past 26 odd years. This can also be left whole and served as a decorated Chocolate Cake.

INGREDIENTS

- 225g sugar
- 45g cocoa
- 110g butter or margarine
- 85g self raising flour
- ½ tsp salt
- 2 eggs, beaten

METHOD

1. Preheat oven to 180°C.
2. Melt butter/margarine over gentle heat, add sugar and remove from heat.
3. Sieve flour, salt and cocoa into the pan and add eggs.
4. Stir well and pour into greased lined 20x20cm shallow square tin.
5. Bake for 25 to 30 mins, allow to cool and cut into squares.

Serves: 9 people

RITA'S APPLE TART

From Rita Molloy, Co. Dublin

Rita baked this apple tart all of her married life, a recipe she learned from Mrs Molloy, her mother-in-law.

INGREDIENTS

- 450g plain flour
- 285g butter or margarine
- 170ml water
- 4 cooking apples

METHOD

1. Preheat oven to 200°C.
2. Sieve the flour, cut up the butter or margarine and rub it together with your fingertips until it looks like bread crumbs.
3. Pour in the water and combine together. Cut a quarter of the pastry and roll it out. Fill with peeled, chopped cooking apples and sprinkle liberally with sugar.
4. Roll out another quarter for the top of the tart. Cut around the edges with the back of a knife and with your fingers flute the edges. Pierce the top of the tart with a fork.
5. Cook in the middle of the oven for 30 to 35 minutes.

Serves: 8–10 people / Makes 2 tarts

ANN KEANE'S PAVLOVA

From Ann Keane, Co. Tipperary

INGREDIENTS

- 8 large egg whites
- 450g caster sugar
- 2 level tsp cornflour
- 2tsp white wine vinegar

For the filling
- 450ml cream – whipped softly
- Strawberries or berries of your liking
- Icing sugar for dusting or chocolate shavings or chocolate sauce for topping

METHOD

1. Preheat the oven to 160°C. Lay non-stick baking parchment on a baking sheet and mark a 23cm circle on it. Do the same for a 18cm circle and again for a 10cm circle.

2. Put the egg whites into a large bowl and whisk until stiff and cloud like. Add the sugar a teaspoonful at a time, whisking well after each addition, until all the sugar has been added.

3. Blend the cornflour and vinegar together and whisk into the meringue mixture. Continue to whisk until the mixture is completely smooth and holds stiff peaks.

4. Spread the meringue out to cover the circles on the non-stick baking parchments, building up the sides so they are higher than the middle.

5. Place in the oven but immediately reduce the temperature to 150°C. Bake for about 1 hour until firm to touch and a pale beige colour. Turn the oven off and allow the Pavlovas to become quite cold while still in the oven. If you keep the oven door closed you will encourage a more marshmallowy meringue. (If you want to use the next day – keep in the oven overnight to set before you put on the cream and berries)

6. Remove the cold Pavlovas from the baking sheet and parchment and slide onto a serving plate. Top with the whipped cream and strawberries, stacking the meringues as you go, then serve.

Serves: 10–12 people

ALMOND CAKE

From Sharon Reid, Volunteer National Office, Dublin

Sharon volunteers with the fundraising team in National Office. This recipe comes from her Father-in-law who turned 92 this year. He shares an early memory:

"Some 86 years ago, when I was a little boy aged six or seven, we were living in a suburb of Paris called Neuilly. On Sundays, we used to go to mass at the local church of Saint Pierre de Neuilly on the other side of the Avenue de Neuilly, now called the Avenue Charles de Gaulle. On the way back we would call at a little pastry shop in a side street to get our Sunday treat. Replacing our usual fruit and cheese for dessert, we often got what was then called a 'gatêau a la pate d'amandes' (an almond paste cake). I have since learned that it is actually called a 'Pithiviers', the name of a town in central France where it was first made in the Eighteenth century."

INGREDIENTS

Pithiviers
- 2 sheets ready made frozen puff pastry (500g)
- 1 egg
- Icing sugar

Almond Cream
- 100g ground almonds
- 50g butter
- 100g sugar
- 1 whole egg
- 1 tbsp rum
- vanilla and almond essence

METHOD

1. Defrost frozen pastry, following the instructions on the pack. This takes about an hour.

2. Prepare the almond cream by mixing the sugar, butter, egg, almonds, vanilla & almond essence, and rum in a food processor until light and runny. Line a shallow 6 inch bowl with cling film and spoon in the mixture. Smooth the top flat and put in the freezer for at least an hour, until stiff.

3. Preheat the oven to 220°C

4. Prepare an egg wash with egg and a tablespoonful of water.

5. On a floured counter, roll out a sheet of pastry. Using a lid or pan as a guide, cut out a disk about 22 to 24cm diameter, wrap it around the rolling pin and unroll on an oiled baking sheet. Once completed keep in the fridge.

6. Roll out the second sheet and cut a disk as before. Remove the first disk from the fridge along with the filling from the freezer, peel off the plastic and place filling in the middle of the disk. Paint a 2 inch border on the edge of the pastry with the egg wash. Carefully place the second pastry disk on top and ease it over the filling smoothing it out on the edges. Moisten the rim and roll back the edges to make them stick. Mark a circle in the centre with a pepper cellar top. Mark out the rim with a knife into strips. Put in the fridge for 20 minutes.

7. Take out of the fridge, brush the whole top surface with egg wash and with the back of a knife draw 3mm deep curves from the middle of the pie to the ends of the strips.

8. Bake at 220°C for 10 minutes, then lower the temperature to 200°C and bake for another 30 minutes. Sprinkle with icing sugar and return to the oven increasing the heat until browned.

Serves: 8 people

VICKY'S CHOCOLATE BISCUIT CAKE

From Sarah Duffy, Dublin

"This recipe was given to me by my best friend's mum Vicky a few years back, when I plucked up the courage to ask her to share it with me!! My family constantly ask me to make it, it never fails to disappoint".

Sarah joined National Office in Blackrock in March 2014. She works part time as secretary to our CEO and assists on Reception. Sarah is always there to lend a helping hand to all departments and is extremely enthusiastic about the work of ASI.

INGREDIENTS

- 225g dairy milk chocolate
- 110g butter
- 185g golden syrup
- 2 heaped tbsp drinking chocolate
- 225g rich tea & digestive biscuits (half and half). Biscuits broken into small pieces

METHOD

1. Melt the chocolate, butter, golden syrup and drinking chocolate. When nearly melted use a whipping motion to combine.
2. Mix in biscuits.
3. Pour into a grease proof dish/tin and press down to compact it.
4. Chill in fridge. Take out of fridge a few hours before serving as it will be rock hard initially.

Serves: 6–8 people

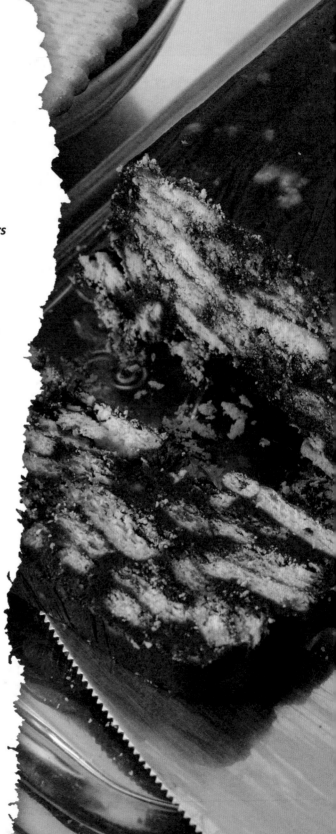

ICE CREAM CHEESECAKE

From Clients of Tredagh Lodge Day Care Centre, Drogheda

Ice Cream cheesecake is one our favourite recipes to make at the centre.

INGREDIENTS

- 20 digestive biscuits
- 115g butter
- 750ml ice cream
- 200g cream cheese
- 250ml fresh cream
- 250g fruit flavoured jelly
- Fruit for decoration (optional)

METHOD

Biscuit base

1. Melt the butter over a low heat
2. Crush the biscuits and mix with the butter
3. Use the mixture to line base of a 23–25cm cheesecake tin, pressing down well
4. Leave biscuit base to set in fridge while preparing topping.

Topping

1. With a hand mixer blend ice cream and cream cheese
2. Add cream and mix well
3. In a separate bowl melt the jelly in microwave, taking care not to allow jelly to boil.
4. As quickly as possible, add melted jelly to ice cream mix and mix thoroughly.
5. Pour over biscuit base & leave to set overnight.

Serves: 10–12 people

BETHANY HOUSE RED VELVET DELIGHTS

Bethany House, Co. Carlow

"These are a favourite with our clients here at Bethany House, and what's not to love about these delicious treats? Speaking with our keen bakers in the centre, they've all tasted these delights and have fond memories of them. Mary received a beautiful red velvet cupcake from her husband with a love heart on top. Maggie remembers baking them for her first grandchild's christening and everyone enjoyed them. While Geraldine admits to not baking them, they are a favourite of hers – satisfying her sweet tooth. We also had some fun recently in-house when Michelle, one of our care workers, brought in some ingredients for us to cook up a batch."

INGREDIENTS

- 200g sugar
- 120ml vegetable oil
- 2 free range eggs
- 240ml buttermilk
- 2 tsp vanilla extract
- 2 tbsp red food liquid colouring – amount will depend on the type of colouring you're using and how red you want them
- 260g plain flour
- 1 tsp baking soda
- 1 tsp salt
- 2 tsp unsweetened cocoa powder
- 120ml hot water

CREAM CHEESE FROSTING
- 225g cream cheese
- 60g softened butter
- 250g icing sugar

METHOD

1. Preheat oven to 200°C.
2. Take a large bowl and add your sugar and oil mixing well.
3. Take the eggs and beat them in a cup. Add the beaten eggs, buttermilk, vanilla extract and food colouring into bowl and mix well.
4. Taking the baking soda and salt mix together with the flour then add to the bowl. Stir in the cocoa powder and finally mix in the hot water.
5. Ensure that all the ingredients are mixed well.
6. Take out your cup-cake cases and fill each ⅔ full with the mixture. Once all the mixture is used, place in your pre heated oven and cook for 20 mins.

Cream cheese frosting

7. Beat cream cheese and butter together.
8. Add in the icing sugar and beat well.
9. Allow cupcakes to cool and then place icing on top of each.
10. Add chocolate sprinkles to decorate if desired.
11. Boil the kettle, make a cuppa sit back relax and enjoy. Yum Yum

Serves: 24 cupcakes

MAURA LAWLOR'S CHRISTMAS PUDDING

From Maura Lawlor, Co. Laois

While everyone dreams of the Christmas feast, as we grow older, we realise the work involved – none more so than my mother, who began her mammoth task of pudding-making in October. To my sister Bernadette, brother Niall, and I, it seemed as though she was making pudding for every member of the Portarlington community. But it was a very special time as the kitchen filled with steam and we were drafted in to help. We sneakily helped ourselves to the fruit and nuts while nobody was looking.

I think the special ingredient was generosity, for my mother never forgot anyone when the pudding list was drawn up. Many years have passed and while we grew up and moved away, Mam always had a homemade pudding for us in December.

This recipe brings back fond memories of the lovely smell of puddings while they steamed for hours on the top of the range that Mam used to have. Thinking back Mam probably would have been better steaming them in the oven but she made so many, she would have needed a much bigger oven. I remember she used to send one to her brother Tom, who lived in Dublin, and before that when he lived in England. There was only the two of them in the family.

As my own children got older, my eldest daughter Lynda looked for one for her house so the tradition continued. My daughter Amy has since taken up the tradition, and has made the pudding but it just isn't the same for some reason. Maybe it is missing Mam's touch. Later this autumn I am going to get the ingredients and get Mam, Amy, Maya and myself working on a pudding for Christmas and, with the help of Mam as the head chef, we surely will create the perfect pudding just like Mam did for so many years!

Mam was diagnosed with Alzheimer's in late 2012 and we have been involved with The Alzheimer Society since February 2013. When a family training course came up in October 2014, myself and my sister Bernadette went along to it and also attended some support group's meetings on occasion.

We get a home carer who comes to my mother a few days a week and makes sure she gets her dinner and she loves the bit of company when she is at home. She goes to day care two days a week which she loves and this is hughly beneficial in keeping her active and getting her out of the house.

I myself became a branch member in 2016 and have been Public Relations Officer for the Laois Branch since early 2018. I am trying to raise awareness and get as much information as possible about the services and supports provided by The Alzheimer Society of Ireland into local papers, Parish Newsletter and websites.

INGREDIENTS

- 55g self-raising flour
- 110g brown sugar
- 110g butter or margarine
- 225g chopped suet
- 2 eggs
- 1 tsp cinnamon
- 350g packet dried fruit mix
- 100g glacé cherries
- 55g chopped almonds
- 110g white breadcrumbs
- 250ml stout
- Half a glass of whiskey

METHOD

1. Beat butter/margarine and sugar together; add the eggs and mix well.
2. Stir in the flour and cinnamon; next add the almonds, fruit, suet and cherries, and mix well.
3. Finally add the breadcrumbs whiskey and stout; stir well. Cover and allow to stand overnight.
4. Next day, transfer to a greased 1lt pudding bowl.
5. Preheat oven to 150⁰C.
6. Put two long strips of tin foil crosswise on worktop. Place roasting tin on foil.
7. Sit pudding bowl into the tin and fill with boiling water to within 1 inch of the top of the tin.
8. Quickly bring the foil around to form a parcel, which should be airtight to prevent steam escaping.
9. Steam for 6 hours.

Serves: 6–8 people

83

BAKED ALASKA

Vera Kennally, Co. Dublin

*"As children, I always remember my mam cooking every
day and there would always be buns, soda bread or my
Dad's favourite, spotted dick. But baked Alaska was a
special for Christmas or Easter but since my dad passed
away nearly 15 years now, my mam's mixer has never
been turned on or indeed any of mam's cooking utensils
– it all stopped when my dad passed. Everything,
especially the smells of cooking, reminded mam of dad
so much, it stopped and I miss it all."*

INGREDIENTS

- 1–2 packs trifle sponge
- 3 egg whites
- 200g caster sugar
- 1 block (568ml) ice cream
- Fruit and some juice, to serve

METHOD

1. Preheat oven to 250C.

2. Beat the egg whites until stiff, then whisk in the caster
   sugar until you have thick, glossy peaks.

3. Lay a piece of the sponge on a baking tray and put the
   block of ice cream on top. Cut the remaining pieces
   of sponge to fit around the ice cream so that it is
   completely covered.

4. Cover everything with the meringue mixture, making
   sure there are no gaps. Bake for 2–5 minutes on middle
   shelf until meringue browns. Serve within 20 minutes.
   Cover with fresh or tinned fruit.

Serves: 8 people

CHOCOLATE CAKE

From Joan O'Connor, Co. Cork

"My Aunt Peggy baked this cake all the time and passed the recipe on to me. I now bake it for the birthdays of all my grandchildren".

INGREDIENTS

- 4 eggs
- 115g sugar
- 115g self-raising flour

Icing
- 225g icing sugar
- 150g softened butter
- 200g block of Cadbury's milk chocolate
- Splash of milk

METHOD

1. Grease 2 non-stick 18–20cm sandwich tins and preheat oven to 180⁰C .
2. Whisk the eggs and sugar together until pale, thick and creamy.
3. Sieve the self-raising flour and add to the mixture. Divide the mixture equally.
4. Bake for 18 minutes, or until light golden brown and slightly springy to the touch.
5. Remove from tins and cool on a wire rack.
6. Melt chocolate in a bowl over a saucepan of hot water, then set aside to cool slightly.
7. Beat the softened butter and sieved icing sugar together and add melted chocolate, mixing well.
8. Spread one side of each cake with icing and sandwich them together.
9. Use remainder of the icing to cover the top and sides of the cake.
10. Use a fork in circular motion to decorate.

Serves: 8–12 people

MUM'S FAMILY CAKE

From Mary Gallagher, Co. Mayo

"When my Mum was a young lady, her Mum used to make what was called a 'Family Cake'. When my Mum got married, she continued to make the same cake. This was made every Friday and she always served it with a generous portion of country butter. It's a lovely cake that was always worth waiting for every Friday evening. I now, in turn, make this cake regularly. It takes only six minutes to prepare. It is delicious for breakfast, school lunches or supper."

INGREDIENTS

- 225g white flour
- 225g wholemeal flour
- 1 tsp baking powder
- 2 tsp cream of tartar
- ½ tsp salt

- 55g sugar
- 110g raisins/sultanas
- 2–3 tsp caraway seeds
- 350ml buttermilk
- 1 egg

METHOD

1. Preheat oven to 220°C .

2. Sieve flour, salt and baking powder together. Add wholemeal flour, dried fruit, sugar and caraway seed.

3. Beat the egg and add to milk. Mix gradually into dry mix to form soft dough. Knead lightly, shape into a round cake, and place on a floured baking tray. Mark the top with a cross and sprinkle with some caraway seeds.

4. Bake for 35 minutes. Cool on wire tray.

Serves: 4–6 people

JEAN'S RHUBARB TART

From Laura Murphy, Co. Dublin

Growing up in the 70s and 80s on the Northside of Dublin in a home full of women – 5 girls, our parents and the German Shepherd dogs, Gypsy and Nessie, was eventful, to say the least.

Aside from our very close family, the lucky few permitted to gain entrance to our mam's kitchen were advised: "be honoured, not any aul Joe gets into my parliamentary parlour".

Prep began on Saturday for the rhubarb tart. Out in her back garden, she would gently pull the rhubarb bundles she lovingly grew – the garden was her pride and joy. And as we all safely sat snuggled up in front of a roaring fire watching Saturday TV, from her kitchen the tap ran as she meticulously washed the long red thick stalks, beheading their green leaves. This was followed closely by chopping and discarding both ends of each stalk. These ruby red freshly-cut stalks lay solider-like and were put to one side for Sunday morning stripping and chopping.

On Sunday, our mam the self-taught baker and cook, sang out her huge warm loving heart as the radiogram blared. Tippy-toeing into the kitchen, I would try not to disturb her. She enjoyed this early time alone in the kitchen doing what she got so much pleasure from, showing us how she loved us through her cooking and baking.

She had an amazing unsung talent she never even knew. Her tarts were sent over to sick neighbours. They were talked about at funerals. She wasn't surrounded by a large group of friends – she had a very small tight group but her way to show she cared was to make two tarts and send them across the road whether they were celebrating or indeed dealing with some sad news.

Glamourous Jean Murphy was so loved then and is so loved even more now by her adoring proud family and beautiful nine grandkids.

MUREX™

INGREDIENTS

- 115g butter
- 225g flour
- Sugar to sweeten
- 6 rhubarb sticks
- A dollop of dance, a pinch of passion, a smidgen of song and lots of love!

METHOD

1. Preheat oven to 200ºC. Lightly grease an oven proof plate.
2. Skin & chop 6 rhubarb sticks for 1 tart.
3. Sieve flour into a bowl & add the butter breaking into the flour using your fingers. If needed, add water and form a soft mound using a knife.
4. Cut the mound in half and taking first piece of mix roll out the pastry to the size of your plate – intermittently turning the pastry, add sprinkles of flour as you turn over to avoid it sticking to your work counter.
5. Lay the flattened pastry mix on the greased plate to form the tart base.
6. Empty the chopped rhubarb on the plate. Sprinkle over sugar to sweeten.
7. Roll out the remaining pastry mix to cover the rhubarb. With water, dampen the sides of the pastry mix base to seal. Place the pastry top over the rhubarb and seal the edges with the back of a knife. With a fork, poke the centre of the pastry lid to allow steam to escape.
8. Bake for approx. 25 to 30 mins
9. Take out to cool and sprinkle some sugar on top.
10. Serve warm with custard, vanilla ice cream or fresh cream

Serves: 4–6 people

RASPBERRY AND FIG MERINGUES

From Louise Lennox, Co. Dublin

"Having watched the pain and heartbreak many of my close friends have gone through caring for and supporting a parent who has Alzheimer's, saddens me deeply. It has opened my eyes to never take my mind or memory for granted so I'm delighted to be able to share a recipe that holds very fond memories for me of baking in my Mum's kitchen many years ago. My earliest memory of baking was making meringues. My favourite part was turning the bowl upside down to check the egg whites had been whisked properly. Sometimes the mixture fell on my head much to my Mum's horror but added to my excitement of making them. Fresh figs and raspberry cream are a lovely combination. The only fruit tree I grow is a fig tree. When in season they are absolutely delicious."

INGREDIENTS

- 2 large egg whites
- Pinch of salt
- 115g caster sugar
- 250mls double cream
- 2 tablespoons icing sugar
- 2 punnets raspberries
- 3 ripe figs

METHOD

1. Preheat the oven to 110ºC. Line a baking tray with baking paper or baking parchment. Don't use greaseproof paper as the meringues will stick to it.

2. Put the egg whites and a pinch of salt into a large clean mixing bowl. Use an electric hand whisk and beat them on high speed for about two minutes until soft peaks form resembling a big fluffy cloud.

3. Continue whisking and start to add in the caster sugar, one tablespoon at a time. Keep beating for 5 seconds between each addition of sugar. When ready, the mixture should be thick and glossy. You should be able to turn it upside down and if whisked properly should defy gravity and stay in the bowl.

4. Spoon the meringue mixture into a piping bag fitted with a star nozzle. Start by piping a dot in the centre of your meringue nest on the baking paper. Then in one continuous motion go around the dot twice to make a bigger circle 2½ inches in diameter and then pipe around the outer circle twice to make the sides. Repeat this to make the remaining meringues leaving plenty of space between them as the meringues expand as they cook.

5. Bake for 2½ hours then turn off the oven and leave the meringue until the oven is completely cold.

6. Semi whip the cream. Wash the raspberries and figs. In a bowl add in ½ the raspberries and icing sugar then mash together with a fork. Fold the raspberry pulp into the cream. Fill the meringue nests with the raspberry cream. Then cut the figs in slices and arrange on top of the cream with the remaining raspberries.

Serves: 14–16 people

SCIENCE OF PERFECT MERINGUES

Before you begin, wash all the bowls and whisks in hot soapy water. The slightest bit of dirt or grease will affect how well the meringues whisk. This is why plastic bowls should be avoided.

Use eggs that are at room temperature – they whisk up much better than eggs taken straight from the fridge. When separating the egg whites, make sure absolutely no egg yolk gets into the bowl as this will also interfere with the quality of whisking. Add a pinch of salt to help break up the protein in the egg whites. They whisk up higher and faster.

It's important to add the sugar slowly, spoon-by-spoon, as it helps the meringues incorporate lots of air and prevents the meringue mixture separating in the oven.

If you don't have a piping bag, use a plastic freezer bag instead and cut the corner off. Or spoon the mixture into rough rounds. Then use the back of a spoon to hollow out the middle.

Meringues are always crisp. If you prefer a softer, more marshmallow texture then make mini Pavlovas. Use the same recipe as above, then after the sugar is added, mix in ½ teaspoon of cornflour and ½ teaspoon of lemon juice. Bake at 150ºC for 1 hour and leave until the oven has cooled.

Egg whites and sugar are both hygroscopic, meaning they attract water. Meringue becomes soggy when refrigerated or stored in a high-humidity environment. This quality also explains the problem called "weeping" or "sweating", in which beads of moisture form on all surfaces of the meringue. Meringues can last a month in an air-tight container. So, you can double this recipe and cook one batch for now and keep one for later.

BAKED
TREATS

MAM'S PORTER CAKE

From John Williams, Co. Tipperary

Memories Last Forever
Dedicated to Mona Williams – a truly wonderful mother.

For years, my mother would cook the most wonderful stews for us and bake Irish soda bread along with cakes and tarts. Recipes passed on from generations of great cooks and bakers in the family. A particular recipe for Porter Cake passed from my grandmother to my mother.

This recipe was not only a favorite of our family but, I believe, a powerful lure for any neighbour coming to pick potatoes or bring in hay. They were greeted with the atmospheric smell of freshly-baked soda bread along with porter cake, and a host of other baked delights. No-one left empty-handed.

Mam always called over her seven boys as she got ready to bake – so that we could help her but also so she could teach us how to bake and cook. A proud and busy mother, laughing and joking with us, singing while she baked. She would push the ingredients around the bowl and when it was time, she would ask 'do ye want a little taste?' Before she finished the sentence, we were all in the bowl with our fingers.

Of course, Mam used Guinness in the porter cake – *'Guinness has all four food groups after all'*. When the porter cake was baked, Mam would pour melted butter over it and you had a choice of custard, cream or ice cream to go along with it.

It was around 2008 or 2009 when we noticed some memory changes in our mother. Following a hip replacement something was not quite right. Mam was diagnosed with Alzheimer's. We felt numb and it was indeed a sucker punch that we struggled to get up from. But help was available, which is a key message.

The Alzheimer Society of Ireland was a great resource for the family as we struggled to come to terms with what was happening to our dear and loved mother. Having information on the stages of Alzheimer's and the care involved – and what help was available – was such a needed and useful thing.

We have lost our Mam in so many different ways; but she is still smiling; she is so physically fit at 80 years young and well looked-after. We now understand that it's not just our Mam who is living with Alzheimer's, so are her family. Thank you to all the incredible resources like ASI, the local Public Health Nurses and all the Alzheimer's carers throughout Ireland.

The smell of Porter Cake is a memory of our Mam that will never fade. Yes, people come and people go but memories do last forever.

INGREDIENTS

- 450g flour
- 225g butter
- 225g sugar
- 450g sultanas
- 2 eggs
- 250ml porter (Guinness), a drop of whiskey optional
- 1 tsp of baking powder
- 55g chopped peel
- ½ teaspoon each of nutmeg & mixed spice

Increase the amounts for a bigger cake. You can add other bits like cherries, raisins, almonds, nuts, etc. for a variation on the porter cake.

METHOD

1. Preheat oven to 190°C
2. Sieve flour, salt & baking powder. Add sugar, nutmeg & spice. Rub in butter finely.
3. Add fruit.
4. Add porter mixed with beaten eggs, and mix thoroughly.
5. Bake in a well-greased tin (20cm round or square) for 1–1.5 hours.
6. Serve when warm with melted butter, or cold with a spread of butter, or melted butter.

Serves: 8 people

RUM CAKE

Bridget Hoey, Co. Clare

INGREDIENTS

Rum Cake:
- 140g plain flour
- 30g cocoa
- Pinch of salt
- 2 eggs, separated
- 2 level tsp baking powder
- 155g soft brown sugar
- 100ml vegetable oil
- 100ml milk
- 1 tsp vanilla essence

Syrup:
- 80ml water
- 65g sugar
- 2 tbsp rum

METHOD

1. Preheat oven to 180°C.
2. Grease a 20cm square or round tin.
3. Sieve the flour, cocoa and baking powder together and mix with the sugar and salt.
4. In a jug, mix the egg yolks with the vanilla essence and milk, then add to the dry ingredients, mixing well.
5. Beat the egg whites stiffly and fold into the mixture.
6. Pour the mixture into the tin and bake for 20–25 minutes. Leave to cool in the tin, pricking the cake a few times with a fork or skewer.

Syrup

7. Boil the sugar and water to dissolve the sugar.
8. When cooled, add the rum and pour over the cooled cake.
9. Leave to soak overnight and decorate with whipped cream.

Serves: 6–8 people

FORGET ME NOT HARVEST LOAF

From Louise Galligan, Co. Meath

A hand-me-down from my mam (that includes my sweet tooth), also loved by Uncle John!

INGREDIENTS

- 110g butter or margarine at room temperature
- 110g caster sugar
- 2 large eggs
- 225g self-raising flour & 1 level tsp mixed spice sieved together
- 30g glace cherries washed & cut into quarters
- 285g mixed dried fruit
- 75ml milk

To decorate: 8 walnut halves, 3 cherries halved

METHOD

1. Preheat oven to 155°C .
2. Brush a 1kg/2lb loaf tin with melted butter or margarine.
3. Place all ingredients in a mixing bowl and beat with a wooden spoon for 2–3 minutes.
4. Place mixture in tin & smooth the top.
5. Bake on the middle shelf of the oven for 1 hour, or until a skewer comes out clean.
6. Leave in tin for 10 minutes & turn out to cool on a wire tray.

Serves: 8 people

95

TREACLE BREAD

From Margaret Leonard, Castlebar, Co. Mayo

"Margaret baked daily for her family of nine. She also baked for her extended family, friends and neighbours. She baked brown bread, white bread, fruit cakes, treacle cakes, porter cakes and potato cakes. She also grew her own rhubarb and won many prizes at all the local agricultural shows. She was very proud of her own home-made butter and won many prizes for it. She never weighed anything. It was 'a fistful of this', 'a pinch of that', and 'a drop' of whatever liquid she used, be it buttermilk, porter or whiskey.

Her family always remember Margaret as 'carrying everything out to perfection'. She always had a treacle cake ready for her family visits on Sundays. This recipe has been taken from notes that Margaret had written down in a copy. Her daughter uses this copy today and the cakes taste as good now as they did then."

INGREDIENTS

- Plain flour – a few fistfuls
- Baking powder – 1 tsp
- Baking soda – 1 tsp
- Treacle – 3–4 tbsp
- Buttermilk – as desired
- Melted margarine – "not much" – her own words.

METHOD

1. Put all dry ingredients into a bowl. Make a well in the centre. Add buttermilk and melted margarine and mix well.

2. Knead all ingredients until it all comes away from the sides of the bowl. Grease and flour a baking tin. Pour all the mixture into the tin.

3. With a knife, make a deep cut into the mixture in the shape of a cross. Also stab the knife in the middle of each quarter.

4. Bake in a moderate oven. Check after 45 minutes by lifting the cake out of the oven and tapping the bottom of the cake with the tips of the fingers. If it sounds hollow, the cake is baked.

5. Turn out on a wire rack to cool. Serve with some home-made country butter.

Serves: 6–8 people

FERGUS' MOTHER'S BROWN BREAD

Fergus Timmons, Co. Offaly

"My mother's brown bread was a staple for us growing up. I come from what was then a typically large Irish family of seven children (two brothers and four sisters). All of us devoured the brown bread pretty much on a daily basis. We would have it for breakfast and also as a snack and in the summer time as an accompaniment to cold foods and salads. And of course I have kept on the tradition of having the brown bread at Christmas Eve after midnight mass, with the freshly cooked ham and mustard! Absolutely delicious. It is so versatile – you can eat it with pretty much anything, or indeed on its own.

When I told my mother that her bread would be featured in the Alzheimer Society's Cookbook she was absolutely delighted. I asked her for her recollections of the bread. The bread recipe, and the baking method, have evolved over the years. Apparently, she used to make it differently – she used to knead it and it was drier. But over the years, that has changed. Now she makes it using the 'wet method', where all the dry ngredients are added to the bowl, before finally adding the egg and the buttermilk until the consistency is just right. The recent additions of the ground Gogi berries and flax provide a richer flavour. I really hope you enjoy making and eating the bread.

I have been with The Alzheimer Society of Ireland for over four years now in my role as Training Manager. I work in the National Office in Blackrock and we have a great team of people working hard in the background to support the delivery of our services around Ireland.

It's a great organisation to work for, and we are all conscious of the importance of our services to support people affected by dementia. In the Training Department we run a course called Insights into Dementia – it is especially for family carers looking after a loved one with dementia. You can get more details on our website www.alzheimer.ie."

INGREDIENTS

- 120g plain flour
- 290g wholemeal flour
- 30g oat bran
- 1 handful of sesame seeds
- 1 handful mixed seeds (pumpkin & sunflower)
- 50g packet Linwoods crushed flax, sunflower, pumpkin, sesame seeds & goji berries or 50g Linwoods Flaxseed (available from most supermarkets or good health food shops)
- 2 level tsp of baking soda
- 1.5 tsp of salt
- 2 tsp of brown sugar
- 1 egg (beaten)
- 500ml of buttermilk

METHOD

1. Pre-heat oven at 175°C.
2. Pour a little sunflower oil (¾ dessertspoon) into the bottom of both baking tins and spread over the bottom of the tin – avoids the bread sticking.
3. Mix all the ingredients in a bowl. Add any excess oil from the loaf tins. Add the beaten egg. Add the buttermilk until the mix is quite wet and drops off the wooden spoon.
4. Pour the mixture into the loaf tins. Even out the top. If you wish, you can sprinkle sesame seeds lightly on top of the mixture.
5. Bake for 45 to 60 minutes. I usually check the bread is baked at about 50 minutes. Check by inserting a skewer into the middle of each loaf. If the skewer comes out clean, the bread is cooked. If the skewer comes out wet, place the loaf back in the oven for 5 minutes.
6. Once baked, remove from the oven. Leave on a tray to cool for 5 minutes. Turn out loaves, it may be necessary to use a plastic knife to cut around the bread when in tin to loosen out for removal.

Serve with real butter, homemade jam or as part of the full Irish breakfast

Serves: Makes 2 1lb loafs

BANANA BREAD

From Briege Duffy, Carrickmacross, Co. Monaghan

"I started off one year ago in Carrickmacross. I brought in this cake as a treat to the service users for a cup of tea and they just loved it – so, I have been bringing it in many days since."

INGREDIENTS

- 255g self-raising flour
- 110g butter/margarine
- 110g sugar
- 110g raisins
- 2 bananas
- 1 tsp vanilla extract
- 2 eggs
- 1 tsp baking powder
- Pinch salt
- 50g walnuts (optional)

METHOD

1. Preheat the oven to 170°C and grease and line a 1kg/2lb loaf tin.
2. Mix the flour, sugar, salt, butter or margarine and raisins together.
3. Beat the eggs and mash the bananas, then add both to the dry mixture
4. Pour into loaf tin and cook in oven for 1 hour or until a skewer comes out clean.

Serves: 8 people

KILKENNY BISCUITS

From Kilkenny Day Care

"It was just like any other afternoon in the centre. Lunch was over, clients and staff were sitting, having a chat. One of the clients, who has been attending the centre for about 18 months and who is always quiet, out of the blue asked: 'does anyone bake their own biscuits anymore?' Two or three of the other clients said they used to love baking their own biscuits and so we came to an agreement to dedicate Friday as our afternoon tea day. We organised ourselves and everyone helped with the task in hand. There is nothing like relaxing and enjoying the fruits of our labour with a lovey cup of tea and a chat."

INGREDIENTS

- 170g butter, softened
- 170g light brown sugar
- ½ tsp vanilla extract
- 3 eggs
- 340g plain flour
- ¾ tsp baking powder
- Pinch of salt

METHOD

1. Preheat oven to 180°C.
2. Cream the butter and sugar with the vanilla extract for 4–5 minutes in a large mixing bowl until light and fluffy.
3. Add the eggs and beat for a few minutes. Sift the flour, the baking powder and the salt. Add the sifted flour mixture to the butter and eggs mixture and beat slowly until the mixture comes together.
4. Use dessert spoon to spoon dollops of the mixture onto a lined baking tray, and flatten them slightly with the back of the spoon. Bake for 12–15 minutes in the oven. Allow to cool and serve.

Serves: Makes approx 28 biscuits

NAN'S TRADITIONAL SCONES

From Ann O'Malley, Co. Mayo

"My mother used to make these scones when I was young. I would rush home from school and have one with a cup of tea every day and it was my little treat. This was of course before cutters existed so she would have to sculpt the scones herself into these wonderful triangles. As time passed she handed the recipe down to me, and now some five decades later, it has stuck with me. It's never let me down and I think it's time to share this family heirloom and let everyone have their special treat."

INGREDIENTS

- 450g self-raising flour
- 55g caster sugar
- 110g butter or margarine
- 1 egg
- 300ml milk
- 55g raisins

METHOD

1. Preheat oven to 200°C.
2. Sieve the flour into a bowl. Stir the sugar and rub in the margarine/butter. Add raisins. Add milk to make light, fairly soft dough.
3. Turn onto a lightly-floured board and knead if necessary to remove any cracks. Roll out lightly into ½ inch thickness.
4. Cut into scones with a 2-inch cutter dipped in flour.
5. Place on pre-heated baking sheet. Glaze scones and bake for 20 minutes. Cool on a wire tray and enjoy!

Serves: makes 24 scones

CLOOTIE DUMPLING

From Laurence Collins, Co. Wicklow

This recipe is originally of Scottish origin and it comes from Laurence Collins, Day Care Manager of Lily of the Valley Day Care in Co. Wicklow.

"I hated waiting for it to cook when I got home from school and my mother had it boiling for an eternity while we salivated – four hours to be exact. She made it in a pillow case! It's actually delicious and a lot more moist than traditional Christmas pudding. My own wife had a good first effort during the Big Snow, but, and don't mention it, if it was "Come Dine With Me" a bit dry and not like my mother's!"

INGREDIENTS

- 500g plain flour
- 200g beef suet
- 250g castor sugar
- 250g raisins
- 250g sultanas
- 1 tsp ground cinnamon
- 1 tsp ground allspice
- 1 tsp ground ginger
- ¼ tsp freshly grated nutmeg
- 3 tsp baking powder
- ½ tsp salt
- 2 large eggs
- 1 bramley apple, peeled and grated
- 3 tbsp black treacle
- 100ml whole milk
- Extra plain flour for dusting

METHOD

1. Bring a very large pot of water to the boil, leave 2–3 inches of water from the top to make sure the dumpling can be accommodated. Equally there needs to be enough water to make sure the dumpling has room to float.

2. Meanwhile, in a large mixing bowl combine all the dry ingredients (flour, sugar, spices, salt, baking powder, dried fruit and beef suet). In another bowl mix the eggs, milk and black treacle together with the grated apple. Then combine the wet mixture with the dry mixture.

3. Dip your dumpling cloot into the boiling pot of water to soak it for a few minutes. Wring it out to remove the excess water.

4. Spread the cloot over a large work surface and dust it fairly generously with plain flour. The wet cloot and flour combine to form a protective glue-like waterproof surface. Make sure the flour reaches far enough to the edges of the cloot so that the flour will cover the whole dumpling .

5. Empty the dumpling mixture on to the cloot and draw up the cloot around it. Tie it with string, wrapping the string twice around. When you tie the cloot, leave a bit of spare room at the top for the dumpling will expand a little. Make sure to cut a generous length of string so you can tie the excess on to the pot handles to suspend the cloot when it is submerged in the water.

6. Put the lid on and keep on a low simmer for 4 hours. When the dumpling is ready, you can lift it out by the string that was attached to the handle.

7. Remove the cloot and transfer the dumpling to a baking tray. Dry the dumpling in a 180°C preheated oven for 15–20 minutes. When you first remove the cloot, you will have a white glutinous skin which covers the surface of the dumpling. After it has been in the oven it will become darker and form a nice crust on the outside of the dumpling.

Serves: 6 – 8 people

SINGING HINNIES

From Edward Jones, Corbally, Limerick

This large tea time scone first became known as a "Singing Hinnie" when a Geordie housewife was baking this scone for tea and on repeatedly being asked by her children if it was ready to eat, her final reply was "No, it's just singing, hinnies". "Hinnies" is a Geordie term of endearment for children.

INGREDIENTS

- ½ lb plain flour
- 50g butter
- 50g lard
- 25g currants
- ½ tsp salt
- 1tsp baking powder
- Milk and sour cream

METHOD

1. Rub Lard gently into flour, add other dry ingredients.
2. Mix to a soft dough with a little milk and sour cream.
3. Roll out and bake both sides on a hot griddle.
4. Take care turning over as they break easily.

Serves: 4–6 people

KATHY'S HEALTHY CRACKERS

Kathy Ryan, Co. Tipperary

Kathy Ryan was diagnosed with younger onset Alzheimer's in January 2014 at the age of 53. Kathy is the mother of two boys (21 and 23) and lives in Cashel, Co. Tipperary. She is the Vice Chair of The Alzheimer Society of Ireland's Irish Dementia Working Group.

"Living with dementia is all about planning. I write lists and nothing happens unless it is in the diary! I have to look after myself, especially now that I am so busy with my advocacy work – and diet is a big part of that. I find if I eat too much processed food, my mind is foggy and so these crackers are a perfect snack. I live alone but I have two dogs, Juno and Bella, and walking them each day means I need a lot of energy. At present I am training for the Camino di Santiago in September and these crackers mean I always have a high-energy, healthy snack handy."

In January Kathy travelled to Bulgaria to collect a European award on behalf of the Irish Dementia Working Group. The day of the award ceremony marked four years since her diagnosis and Kathy commented that, at that dark moment, she would never have imagined the rich opportunities that participation in the Working Group have opened up for her.

INGREDIENTS

- 75g sunflower seeds
- 65g chia seeds
- 45g flaxseeds
- 20g sesame seeds
- 20g pumpkin seeds
- 2 tsp fennel seeds
- 1 ½ tsp sea salt
- 3 tbsp coconut oil
- 1 tsp dried thyme
- 200ml boiling water

METHOD

1. Preheat your oven to 170°C and line a baking tray with non-stick baking paper.
2. Mix all the dry ingredients together in a mixing bowl.
3. Add the coconut oil to the boiling water so it melts.
4. Once melted, add the dry ingredients and mix well to form a dough.
5. Pour the mixture into the lined baking tray and spread out with a spatula.
6. Place a second sheet of non-stick baking paper on top of the cracker blanket and press down to make the mixture thinner to cover the entire tray.
7. Remove the top piece of baking paper and bake the crackers for 30 minutes.
8. Bake until crispy and golden brown.
9. Turn off the oven and leave to cool fully and dry out before dividing into squares or rectangles for serving.

Serves: 12 crackers

PAPA'S TEA BRACK

From Maria Ní Bhuachalla, Co. Dublin

"When my grandfather, Papa, first developed Alzheimer's disease, he sometimes used to stay with us. As often happens with Alzheimer's patients, entertaining Papa was often a challenge but we soon found that cooking was one of his favourite things to do. Tea brack was the perfect recipe to make with Papa because of the memories he would have of warm, freshly-baked tea brack, smothered in butter. Now, whenever my own mother makes this tea brack, it brings back fond memories of Papa and baking with him."

INGREDIENTS

- 110g raisins
- 110g currants
- 110g sultanas
- 55g mixed candied peel (or you can use a 375g bag of mixed dried fruits and candied peel instead of all of the above).
- 110g demerara sugar
- 140ml hot tea
- 55g walnuts, roughly chopped
- 1 egg, lightly beaten
- 225g self-raising flour

METHOD

1. Place all the fruits, including the candied peel, in a bowl.
2. Dissolve the sugar in the tea and pour over the fruits. Cover the bowl and leave to soak for 15–20 minutes.
3. Preheat the oven to 170ºC.
4. Add the egg to the fruit.
5. Sift in the flour and add the nuts, before mixing well.
6. Pour the mixture into a 1lb loaf tin, lined with baking parchment.
7. Place the tin in the middle of the oven and bake for 1¼–1½ hours, or until they feel springy in the centre.
8. Turn out onto a wire rack to cool.
9. Wait until cool for easy cutting, but warm tea brack is so much tastier!

Serves: makes 1 loaf

HEALTHY MUFFINS

From Julia Brennan, KBC

"At KBC we are partnered with The Alzheimer Society of Ireland. The ASI was selected as our chosen charity of choice, voted by employees in 2017. As part of our partnership, we complete skills sharing, support national campaigns, fundraise locally and supply digital solutions. Our employees lead our partnership developing multiple fundraising opportunities, volunteering at events and creating much-needed awareness for The Alzheimer Society of Ireland (ASI) and their services. Our flagship event, Hub2Hub, was an employee-led, bespoke initiative. This initiative saw over 70 run a 600km, non-stop relay race visiting all KBC hubs across Ireland over 3 days and 2 nights. Staff raised over €50,000 from sponsorship and the bank matched donations, bringing the total raised to over €100,000 in aid of our ASI partnership. Julia Brennan who works in finance with KBC, is not only a baking guru, but is passionate about supporting our charity partner so she was delighted to contribute to this worthy cause."

INGREDIENTS

- 1 egg
- 100g porridge oats
- 100g flour sieved
- 200ml milk
- 100ml water
- 50g desiccated coconut
- 100g mixed seeds
- 100g sultanas
- 100g chopped nuts
- 50g cranberries
- 100g grated mature cheese
- 1 tsp cinnamon

METHOD

1. Preheat the oven to 190°C.
2. Whisk the egg, milk and water together in a jug.
3. Sieve the flour into a big bowl and add all the other dry ingredients.
4. Add the egg and milk to the bowl and mix together.
5. The mixture should be relatively wet and if it is too dry, add more milk or water.
6. Spoon the mixture into muffin cases, well-greased muffin tins, or a well-greased cake tin and bake for 30–35 mins.
7. When baked, leave to cool for 10–15 minutes before loosening the edges with a plastic knife (if not using paper cases), then turn out onto a cooling rack to cool completely. If using paper cases, leave to set in the cases until completely cool; they tend to stick to the paper while still warm.
8. Make a cup of tea and enjoy!

Serves: Makes approx. 18 muffins

GRANNY SMITH'S SODA BREAD

Davina Smith, Co. Dublin

Davina works in the training department in the National office but also trained in Ballymaloe Cookery School and is a qualified nutritional therapist. A woman of many talents! Davina very kindly offered her time to this project and tested many of the recipes featured in this book.

Our family was 'bread and buttered' on this memories evoking Granny's soda bread. Her soda bread would welcome any visitor to the house straight from the open range oven. My father came from a family of 13 from Co. Monaghan and this bread played a major part in their daily diet.

Memories of visiting and summer holidays at Callowhill and the smell of freshly baked bread accompanied with laughter and chats galore. Boiled eggs and soda bread was a daily ritual for my uncles on the farm and for all staying. Granny would know exactly how everyone liked their eggs: soft, hard or in between plus how much butter too on the bread! Her tradition lives on."

INGREDIENTS
- 450g of plain flour
- ½ level tsp of bread soda
- 300–600ml of buttermilk

METHOD

1. Preheat oven to 230°C.
2. Sieve flour and bread soda into a bowl. Make a well in the centre and pour 300ml of milk in. Using one hand, stir with outstretched fingers from the centre to the side of the bowl.
3. Make into soft dough.
4. Turn onto a lightly floured board. Very lightly kneed. Turn over to smooth side and shape into a round approx. 3–4cm deep.
5. Add to a floured tray.
6. Cut a deep cross into the top of the dough.
7. Bake in a pre-heated oven at 230°C for 15 minutes. Turn down to 200°C for 30 minutes.
8. Check if cooked by tapping underneath the tin and hearing a hollow sound.
9. Serve with butter and enjoy.

Serves: makes 1 loaf

SPOTTED DICK

From Christina 'Dina' Watkins, Co. Offaly

Dina is a client of The Alzheimer Society of Ireland's Day Dare Service in Birr since Nov 2017. She attends three days a week and likes it, as it's quiet, very friendly and she gets individual attention. Below is her story behind her recipe for spotted dick.

"When my twin, Nell, and I were 6 or 7 years old, my mother Julia used to take the long journey from Dowras (Fivealley, Birr) on her high nellie bicycle to her home village of Lusmagh and then on to Victoria Lough on the Shannon. Julia's family were the lough-keepers. My father would encourage her to leave early morning and be back during daylight as he was nervous of her returning in the dark. Julia would have things to organise before departing – so it would be one o'clock when she'd head off ensuring we had our chores done.

Daddy would see her as far as Galross Cross and, later that evening, meet her on the way back. We knew what daddy had planned for us when Mammy left. He took out the mixing bowl that mammy used to make bread in. But he had a twist on his bread – he would add around 5 cups of flour, 2–3 tsp of bicarbonate of soda, 3 tsp of sugar, half a jug of buttermilk – and then, he would add 1 cup of sultanas which was like chocolate to us!

He would mix it all together and then empty the lot onto a floured table, kneed the dough into a circle, cut into four and then place into the baker and put the lid on. The hot coals were then put on the lid and it was left to cook for 45 minutes. The smell of the 'spotted dick' cooking would make our mouths water – during rationing in Ireland from 1941 to 1946, sugar, sweets and all things nice for children were in short supply.

Amy my older sister, John my brother, my twin Nell and myself would be so excited on those days as we would have to eat the 'spotted dick' on that day before Mammy returned – this was no problem!

When it was baked, daddy would get the butter which Mammy would have churned before she left for Lusmagh. It was our secret, making it more exciting for the days when mam went to Lusmagh and we were never upset or lonely when she left.

My father taught this recipe to his three girls. I made the 'spotted dick' for my own children every week when they were kids. It never lasted long as it was shared between my four daughters and four sons but on the odd occasion they had a slice or two in their school lunchbox the next day.

Dina passed the recipe onto her own children. Mary, Dina's eldest daughter, makes it for her children who also love it, although Mary's kids still say Granny's is better."

INGREDIENTS

- 5 cups of flour
- 2–3 tsp of bicarbonate of soda
- 3 tsp of sugar
- Half a jug of buttermilk (approx. 600ml)
- 1 cup of sultanas

METHOD

1. Preheat oven to 180°C.

2. Mix all the ingredients together and then empty the lot onto a floured table, knead the dough into a circle, cut into 4.

3. Bake for 45 minutes or until golden and a skewer inserted into the centre comes out clean. Cover with a tea towel and stand for 20 minutes. Serve warm or toasted, with butter.

4. Dina used to place the dough into the baker with the lid on. The hot coals were then put on the lid and it was left to cook for 45 minutes.

Serves: 4 people

ELLEN'S BLACKCURRANT JAM

From Anne O'Connor, Co. Wexford

"This very simple recipe has been passed on to me by my mother-in-law who loved making jam. She was diagnosed with dementia and passed on a few years later. She would be very proud to know her recipe is being carried on, shared and enjoyed. I have made this jam with my clients for the past few summers with my own homegrown fruit – and only last week one of my clients asked 'when are we going to make that lovely jam again?'"

INGREDIENTS

- 1kg blackcurrants – washed with stalks removed
- 2kg sugar – slightly warmed on a tray in oven
- 1.2ltrs of water

METHOD

1. Wash and sterilize 8 x 1lb jam jars warmed in oven to put boiling jam into.

2. Place fruit and water into a saucepan and bring to the boil, then simmer until fruit is softened. This takes around 35–45 minutes.

3. Mash fruit with a masher, then add slightly warmed sugar and stir in gently. When all sugar has dissolved, bring to the boil and boil contents until mixture slightly thickens and starts to stick lightly to the sides of the saucepan (roughly 20 minutes). At this stage, have a saucer in the fridge cold and, removing froth from the top of boiling liquid, put some jam on saucer to cool for 1 minute. When it wrinkles after pushing your finger through, the jam is ready.

4. Put jam into warmed jars and seal tightly, label and date. Enjoy.

Serves: 8 Jars

GRANNY TRIXIE'S HOMEMADE LEMONADE

Trixie Mc Garry, Co. Longford

"This recipe goes back to when my mother was a child growing up in Dublin in the 1930s. It was a treat in the summertime. When I was growing up in Longford in the 1970s, we knew that summer had arrived when Trixie made the first batch of the season and all the children around our block would flock into our garden for Mrs McGarry's lemonade. Needless to say, a batch never lasted too long. She would be back down to the medical hall on the lower main street to get her supply of citric acid – enough to last the summer. Many years later I renamed her lemonade – Granny Trixie's homemade lemonade – which can be bought in my café in Longford and remains her family's favourite to this day."

INGREDIENTS

- 3kg sugar
- 120g of citric acid
- 2lt water
- 8 lemons grated and juiced

METHOD

1. Pour all ingredients into a saucepan and boil until the sugar is dissolved. Fill jars and cap off while lemonade is hot so it creates a seal on the jar. Shelf life 6 months.

2. Once you open the bottle, keep refrigerated and use within a week.

Serving suggestions: as it's a cordial, use a cap-full per glass.

It's delicious with ice and water or to give it an extra special taste, use sparkling water, it's delicious. It's also delicious poured over a bowl of vanilla ice-cream.

If you are feeling under the weather, it's ideal as a hot lemon drink or add a dash of whiskey – purely for medicinal purposes!

Serves: Makes lots of cordial!

MEASUREMENT CONVERSION

WEIGHTS

Metric	Imperial
15g	½ oz
25g	1oz
40g	1½oz
50g	2oz
75g	3oz
100g	4oz
150g	5oz
175g	6oz
200g	7oz
225g	8oz
250g	9oz
275g	10oz
300g	11oz
350g	12oz
375g	13oz
400g	14oz
425g	15oz
450g	1 lb
550g	1¼lb
700g	1½lb
800g	1¾lb

VOLUMES

Metric	Imperial
25ml	1 fl oz
50ml	2 fl oz
75ml	3 fl oz
100ml	3½ fl oz
150ml	5 fl oz
200ml	7 fl oz
300ml	10 fl oz
450ml	15 fl oz
600ml	1 pint

OVEN TEMPERATURES

Gas Mark	Celsius	Fahrenheit
1	140 C	275 F
2	150 C	300 F
3	170 C	325 F
4	180 C	350 F
5	190 C	375 F
6	200 C	400 F
7	220 C	425 F
8	230 C	450 F
9	240 C	475 F

RECIPE Nº.

. . . .

INGREDIENTS

RECIPE No.

INGREDIENTS

RECIPE №.

．．．

INGREDIENTS

RECIPE No. . . . .

INGREDIENTS